foreword by DR. ERWIN LUTZER

friendly fire

WHY IS GOD SHOOTING AT ME?

BY WILLIAM G. JOHNSON
& DON COUWENHOVEN

BOOKS BY LEADERSHIP RESOURCES

Connecting With One Another Series

These devotional Bible studies are designed for personal growth as well as classes and small groups. Each book contains a 9-week discussion guide.

The Path of Joy: Enjoying Intimacy with God
by Marnie Carlson

Friendly Fire: Why Is God Shooting at Me?
by William G. Johnson and Don Couwenhoven

Changed: Experiencing God's Transforming Power
(Also available in Chinese)
by Bill Mills

Naked & Unashamed: Recapturing Family Intimacy
(Also available in Spanish and Chinese)
by Bill Mills

A Quiet Heart: Discovering Peace & Power at Jesus' Feet
by Carla Jividen Peer

Beyond Independence: Reclaiming Our Life Together in Christ
by Bill Mills

Pursuing God: Finding Our Fullness in Christ
(Also available in Chinese)
by Bill Mills

Shoulder to Shoulder: How God Builds Spiritual Men
(Also available in Chinese)
by Bill Mills

The Day of the Lord! Preparing to Meet the Bridegroom
by Bill Mills

The Blessing of Benjamin:
Living in the Power of Your Father's Approval
by Bill Mills and Peter Luisi-Mills

Connecting With God for Growth and Ministries Series

These devotional Bible studies will help you grow in your relationship with the Lord and in your ministry.

Adequate! How God Empowers Ordinary People to Serve
(Also available in Chinese)
by Bill Mills

Language of the Heart: Knowing Joy and Communion in Prayer
by Bill Mills

Finishing Well in Life and Ministry: God's Protection from Burnout
(Also available in Spanish and Chinese)
by Bill Mills and Craig Parro

Unlikely Warriors: Our Call to Invade the Darkness
by Craig Parro

Inductive Bible Study Series

These Bible study helps will enable you to grow in your understanding of the Scriptures and in your preparation for teaching.

Proverbs: Lessons for the Growing Years (for Jr/Sr High)

Jonah: Inductive Bible Study

Philippians: A Family Bible Study

Ruth: The Romance of Redemption

Inductive Bible Study Handbook
by Dennis Fledderjohann

A Servant Series

Each book contains 21 articles from many well-known authors. Great library resources!

Marriage, Parenting & Forgiveness
Reconciliation, Fellowship & the Grace of God

You may order our books and Bible conference CDs on our web site:
www.LeadershipResources.org

Fourth Printing—2008

Copyright © Leadership Resources 1995, 12575 Ridgeland Avenue, Palos Heights, IL 60463.

Unless otherwise indicated Scripture quotations are taken from the *Holy Bible,* English Standard Version, copyright © 2001 by Crossway Bibles, a division of Good News Publishers. All rights reserved. Used by permission.

Scripture quotations marked NASB are taken from the *New American Standard Bible,* © 1960, 1962, 1963, 1968, 1971, 1972, 1973, 1975, 1977 by The Lockman Foundation. Used by permission.

Scripture quotations marked NIV are taken from *The Holy Bible: New International Version,* © 1973, 1978, 1984 by The International Bible Society.

Scripture quotations marked NKJV are taken from the *New King James Version,* © 1982 by Thomas Nelson, Inc.

Scripture quotations marked *The Message*: © 1993, 1994, 1995, 1996, 2000, 2001, 2002, by Eugene H. Peterson.

This book, or portions thereof, may not be reproduced without written permission of Leadership Resources International.

THIS MINISTRY IS DEDICATED TO

The Glory of God
The Honor of His Word
The Building Up of the Body of Christ

Though he slay me, I will hope in him ...

Job 13:15a

Table of Contents

Foreword — 10
Preface — 11
Introduction — 15

Act I
1. The Conflict Begins — 19

Act II
2. Eliphaz, the Shame-Seller — 31
3. Bildad, the Oversimplifier — 53
4. Zophar, the Zealot — 71
5. The Battlepoint — 87
6. God, Why Are You Shooting at Me? — 105
7. Resurrection Glory and the Believer's Reward — 123
8. The Mental and Spiritual Conflict — 147

Act III
9. Effective Counseling — 169
10. Hope in the Redeemer — 187

Act IV

11. Job Meets God   209
12. Brokenness   227

Bibliography   237
Scripture Index   239
Leadership Resources   245

FOREWORD *by*
Dr. Erwin W. Lutzer

*Senior Pastor, The Moody Church
Chicago, Illinois*

We've all found ourselves on the slope of a question mark wondering, "God, why me?"

In this book Bill Johnson shows us that he has felt our pain and understood our questions. And through the life of Job, we learn insights into God's dealings with us.

Friendly Fire is an excellent title, reminding us that our trials do come from the hands of Someone who loves us. And the content between the covers of this book will be a blessing, giving new insights into an age-old problem. When things are against us, we are reminded that they might actually be *for* us.

Bill invites us not merely to learn from Job, but to work through our own understanding of how God treats us when we find an arrow in our own hearts.

This is both a textbook and a Bible study. You will be guided into your own understanding of this timeless masterpiece. We can be encouraged to learn that the God of Job is still with us.

Erwin W. Lutzer
1997

Preface

F*riendly Fire* is both a textbook and a Bible study. Questions written for each chapter are located at the end of the book and are for individual and small group use. After the Questions a section entitled Don's Reflections has been added by the co-author. After sitting under Pastor Johnson's teaching and ministry for over 20 years and with his untimely (from our perspective) entrance into glory, God has laid upon my heart the desire to continue the vision Pastor Johnson had in regards to sharing the wonderful, but heart wrenching, story of Job. It is not my intent to detract in any way from Pastor's work but to supplement and encourage readers by sharing how the sovereign hand of God can sustain us through pain, anger and disappointment.

This Bible study is intended to be done on a regular basis—one chapter a week for twelve weeks. There is, of course, room for flexibility, depending upon the needs of the person or groups using this book.

Study and preparation are essential before meaningful discussions can take place. There is very limited value to entering into a group discussion if your only preparation has been to casually read the chapter.

As questions guide you into Scripture passages, ask God to reveal His truths to you. As with all of Scripture, the reader is encouraged to read, reread, re-reread and read again to try to ascertain what the inspired author is intending to convey. Be encouraged to share with your group any insights or questions which you may have. It is the prayer of your friends at Leadership Resources International that by looking at the life of Job, God will lead you to changes of eternal significance in *your* life.

In His Grace,

Don Couwenhoven

There was a man in the land of Uz whose name was Job, and that man was blameless and upright, one who feared God and turned away from evil.

Job 1:1

Introduction

Almost everyone knows about Job. He was the ancient agricultural entrepreneur who had multiple tragedies hit him in such quick succession that we hardly have time to feel with him the depth of his despair.

We know that he has a reputation for patience, or better, perseverance. We know that his situation was remedied so well that he was considerably better off in the end than in the beginning.

However, most readers of the book recall only the prologue, (chapters 1 and 2) and the epilogue (chapters 38 through 41). This is a great loss because the drama of Job (chapters 3 through 37) is the meat of the book.

This ancient play is gripping and richly rewarding to those who are willing to go deeper into the dialogue. The implications of the contest in Heaven and Job's conflict with his well-meaning friends are often lost. His personal struggles and the astonishingly skillful counseling of a younger friend are overlooked. The casual reader will pick up on a few well-known cliché verses, but

Friendly Fire

the profound answer to the question of "Why do bad things happen to good people?" is missed.

I have a passion that people, especially Christians, come to know and understand the message of the book and its sound wisdom for living life well. Whether we are being crushed by suffering or comfortably "successful," Job teaches us all.

It is important to remember that Job is the oldest book in the Bible. Genesis was not written first, but Job. Moses wrote his five books in the 14th century, B.C. The description of the times in which Job lived fit the Patriarchal period, the days of Abraham—2000 years before Christ; 500 years before Moses. Although we cannot be certain, I believe that Elihu was the author and that he wrote this drama shortly after the events occurred. The fact that Job was the earliest of Biblical writings gives it special "weight." Obviously, God determined to reveal the basic truths of Job to a suffering, struggling humanity at the very beginning of His written revelation.

During our early 40's, my wife and I struggled through a time of family crisis. Before that time I had read Job in a perfunctory manner. In seminary it was assigned reading. As a pastor, reading the Bible through each year was part of my reading plan. Frankly, I skimmed through the arguing of Job and his friends, noting a few favorite passages. I knew, from a New Testament reference, that Job was considered an example of patience. However, I must confess that I thought he was a whiner and not a very good testimony as he expressed his anger at God. However, that was before pain drove me to search for deeper answers.

It was in God's providence that Dr. William Hulme, professor of pastoral psychology at the Lutheran Seminary in St. Paul, Minnesota, delivered a series of lectures on the book of Job at Bethel Seminary during their annual Founder's Week. As my

Introduction

wife and I listened, he opened up the whole drama of Job and made sense of the perplexing middle chapters.

Dr. Hulme's lessons, contrasting the pious emotional dishonesty of Job's friends with Job's ability to be honest with his feelings, gave me hope. I saw that Job came through suffering, shame, disappointment and pain—not just *somehow*, but *triumphantly*. This, to me, is reason enough for God to give the book of Job *first* into the experience of mankind.

I began to understand the freedom of living "under Grace" instead of "under the gun"; i.e., *trying* to be acceptable to God. I determined to share the freedom I was finding with my congregation and anyone else who might be open to it. (A church, like a person, can be theologically sound but emotionally unwholesome.)

Before personally suffering losses that were beyond my understanding, I would have said, "If it is doctrinally sound, it will *automatically* be healthy emotionally." The Word of God *is* sound teaching. I am learning, however, that we pastors and Bible teachers can, like Job's friends, use the truth of God's Word to manipulate, to intimidate, and even to abuse.

God's truth, as presented in the Book of Job, is not only healing for a deeply despairing person, but in it there is also solid Biblical guidance for helping others.

I would like to imagine that I am ushering you down to the best seats in the theater, a few rows back from the stage, near the center aisle. As we take our seats for this drama, the lights are lowered, the curtain is raised and the first scene introduces us to the central figure: Job.

And the Lord said to Satan, "Have you considered my servant Job, that there is none like him on the earth, a blameless and upright man, who fears God and turns away from evil?"

                Job 1:8

Act I

1

The Conflict Begins

The Key: The explanation for life on earth with its anguish and adversity lies in a recognition of the cosmic conflict in the spiritual realm.

SCENE 1: PROLOGUE

There was a man in the land of Uz whose name was Job, and that man was blameless and upright, one who feared God and turned away from evil. There were born to him seven sons and three daughters. He possessed 7,000 sheep, 3,000 camels, 500 yoke of oxen, and 500 female donkeys, and very many servants, so that this man was the greatest of all the people of the east. His sons used to go and hold a feast in the house of each one on his day, and they would send and invite their three sisters to eat and drink with them. And when the days of the feast had run their course, Job would send and consecrate them, and he would rise early in the morning and offer burnt offerings according to the

Friendly Fire

> number of them all. For Job said, "It may be that my children have sinned, and cursed God in their hearts." Thus Job did continually. (Job 1:1-5)

Some substantial fellow, this farmer: blameless, upright and "filthy" rich. He is godly and the greatest man in his part of the world.

However, Job's family was a concern to him. His adult children were beyond his ability to control. Their birthday parties seem to have been more than just simple little "get-togethers."

Job's post-party offerings of a sacrifice for each of his children gives us an endearing insight into his character. He was more troubled by the possibility of their "sinning in their hearts" than by any particular behavior of celebration.

SCENE 2: THE CONFLICT IN HEAVEN

The stage lights dim; the curtain falls, then rises and the scene is changed. The action now shifts to Heaven. The angels, like soldiers, are presenting themselves in review before God. Though uninvited, Satan joins them to spoil the parade.

> Now there was a day when the sons of God came to present themselves before the LORD, and Satan also came among them. The LORD said to Satan, "From where have you come?" Satan answered the LORD and said, "From going to and fro on the earth, and from walking up and down on it." (Job 1:6-7)

(The background music of our play turns ominous here.)

> And the LORD said to Satan, "Have you considered my servant Job, that there is none like him on the earth, a blameless and upright man, who fears God and turns away from evil?" (Job 1:8)

Why would God challenge Satan regarding Job? We will see. The answer is at the root of God's purpose in choosing to give this book to the world.

The Conflict Begins

> Then Satan answered the LORD and said, "Does Job fear God for no reason? Have you not put a hedge around him and his house and all that he has, on every side? You have blessed the work of his hands, and his possessions have increased in the land. But stretch out your hand and touch all that he has, and he will curse you to your face." And the LORD said to Satan, "Behold, all that he has is in your hand. Only against him do not stretch out your hand." So Satan went out from the presence of the LORD. (Job 1:9-12)

"Why should he not honor You; look at the way You take care of him!" sneers Satan. The gauntlet is down; Satan accepts the challenge. I love that phrase, *"Do not lay a finger..."* God will let Satan go only so far and no more.

Scene 3: Devastation

A change of scene and the play action flashes back to earth. We know what went on in Heaven and why Job's troubles began. We know what is behind the terrible reversal of Job's fortunes. We know—but, of course, Job does not.

This audience prescience is what is so exciting about drama. The audience knows things that the participants do not. We fear for them. We want to cry out to them, warn them, help them somehow.

Satan strikes quickly as Job's children are having one of their parties. A messenger comes to Job, crying:

> "The oxen were plowing and the donkeys feeding beside them, and the Sabeans fell upon them and took them and struck down the servants with the edge of the sword, and I alone have escaped to tell you." While he was yet speaking, there came another and said, "The fire of God fell from heaven and burned up the sheep and the servants and consumed them, and I alone have escaped to tell you." (Job 1:14-16)

Friendly Fire

While Job is reeling from these multiple calamities, another messenger comes and says,

> While he was yet speaking, there came another and said, "Your sons and daughters were eating and drinking wine in their oldest brother's house, and behold, a great wind came across the wilderness and struck the four corners of the house, and it fell upon the young people, and they are dead, and I alone have escaped to tell you." (Job 1:18-19)

Job's response is primitive and magnificent. He tears his robe. He shaves his head in mourning. He falls to the ground and worships God, saying something so beautiful, so memorable that it has become imbedded into the cultural language of civilized humanity:

> And he said, "Naked I came from my mother's womb, and naked shall I return. The LORD gave, and the LORD has taken away; blessed be the name of the LORD." (Job 1:21)

Perhaps this touches a chord in you. In a time of grave difficulty, you experience a powerful sense of the presence of the Lord. You do not *feel* like praising God, but you *choose* to do so. God meets your heart. Something in you breaks and you are able to say, "Yes, Lord." Such is a beautiful testimony; you experience a joy, sensing that God is pleased; like Job, you do not accuse God of wrong-doing.

SCENE 4: SATAN'S SECOND SHOT

So far, so good, but now comes a new test. The scene moves back to Heaven and another review of the angels before God. (These changing scenes make us aware that the drama of the Book of Job is played out on two levels: One is the conflict in Heaven between God and Satan while the other is the trial of Job with his circumstances and misguided friends on earth. We will become

The Conflict Begins

aware that these two levels interact with each other and that this interaction is inextricably part of life for every one of us.)

As the angelic army gathers before the Lord in formal review, the fallen angel Satan comes in among them and presents himself. The Lord God challenges His enemy again:

> And the LORD said to Satan, "Have you considered my servant Job, that there is none like him on the earth, a blameless and upright man, who fears God and turns away from evil? He still holds fast his integrity, although you incited me against him to destroy him without reason." Then Satan answered the LORD and said, "Skin for skin! All that a man has he will give for his life. But stretch out your hand and touch his bone and his flesh, and he will curse you to your face." (Job 2:3-5)

I inwardly cringe at the Lord's reply to Satan:

> And the LORD said to Satan, "Behold, he is in your hand; only spare his life." So Satan went out from the presence of the LORD and struck Job with loathsome sores from the sole of his foot to the crown of his head. (Job 2:6-7)

Note that God would not strike Job as Satan suggested. Job's troubles were not initiated by God, but they did come through the hedge of protection that God had around him. God opened that hedge so Satan could move against Job in these calamities.

SCENE 5: DISEASE

Our drama shifts to earth again.

Sitting on a pile of ashes, Job takes a piece of broken pottery and scrapes himself. Then comes the culmination of calamities. His wife, understandably devastated by their losses, lashes out in despair:

> Then his wife said to him, "Do you still hold fast your integrity? Curse God and die." (Job 2:9)

Friendly Fire

(Are you still trying to sound like a good Christian?)

Job has lost his business, his wealth, his status, his children, his health, and now, as far as any support is concerned, it looks as though he has lost his wife also. However, he refuses to cave in and rail against God:

> But he said to her, "You speak as one of the foolish women would speak. Shall we receive good from God, and shall we not receive evil?" In all this Job did not sin with his lips. (Job 2:10)

How typical! My wife Marian may be hurting over something painful that is happening to us, and, always the preacher, I, like Job, will have some word of Scripture or some wonderful word of wisdom and will feel rather self-righteous about it. I can identify with this hurting couple. Job's wife is thinking, "What has happened to our lives? I have lost my children, and now you will not even let me express my pain and rage." Job is trying to hold things together and maintain a positive attitude.

This couple speaks to every family who is in deep pain. It is hard to think of someone who has had it worse. Yet we all have despaired for less. I know that I can take almost anything as long as Marian does not weaken. If she's right there with me and respects me, I'm like a lion. But if she begins to slide… (We sometimes say to each other, "Isn't it fortunate that when one of us is down, the other is up and vice-versa?") Obviously, Job's situation is much more serious than just "havin' a bad day." Then, again, have you noticed that regarding "feelings," life's *little* reversals seem as painful as the great ones.

The Conflict Begins

GROUP STUDY GUIDE
AND PERSONAL APPLICATION

1. From the opening verses of the book of Job, we learn much about this great man of ancient history. List several words which best describe Job's character.

2. Job displayed a great responsibility toward his ten children. What do these verses tell us he did for his sons and daughters? Why did he do it? If Job were living today, what kind of things might he do for his children? How do you bring your children before the Lord?

3. God chose to share with the world His conflict with Satan. Because Satan could not deny Job's godliness, he questioned Job's motive for living a blameless life. What does Satan suggest as Job's motive for godliness?

4. Job was an exemplary person, blameless before God, who did nothing to deserve the suffering he experienced; however, few people, if any, have suffered more than he did. Describe Job's first losses. What was his response to such personal devastation?

5. In his worship of God, Job spoke the words found in Job 1:21, suggesting that his loss resembled his birth and death. Read this verse again and write in your own words the message Job was giving.

6. Regardless of our circumstances, we can choose to praise God. Think of a time when you faced a crisis. What was your first response to your trouble? In what ways could you have changed your response using Job's example?

Friendly Fire

7. Describe the second test which came to Job. Who initiated this trouble? What did Satan predict that Job would do this time? How did Job respond to his failing health?

8. Imagine that you are Job's wife. You, too, have just lost all your children and wealth. Besides, your spouse, though still alive, is sitting in misery in a heap of ashes outside the city. How would you feel if you were in her place? What did she tell Job to do? Discuss whether or not you feel that Job's wife was justified in her suggestion.

9. Job's wife advised him to curse God, which is exactly what Satan had predicted he would do. How did Job reply to his wife? What did his quick response indicate about his relationship to God?

10. Can you recall a time in your life which seemed so bad that you doubted that you could ever be happy again? Were you tempted to accuse God of wrongdoing? Could you sense the presence of the Lord in a special way?

Don's Reflections

As we begin our sojourn through this amazing gift of inspired Scripture, I would like to quote from Randy Paush, a gifted teacher, author and inspirational speaker, who, at this writing is probably in his last weeks of life. Mr. Paush is dying after a long fight with pancreatic cancer. His journey has been closely followed by ABC and Diane Sawyer and recorded in his book titled, *The Last Lecture: A love story for your life*. Ms. Sawyer's interview with Randy Paush aired April 9, 2008. One of Randy's statements in that interview was, "Don't tell people how to live their lives, tell them stories." (Note: Randy died July 25, 2008)

As much as possible and appropriate, I have endeavored to use real life stories along with God's Word to illustrate God's sov-

The Conflict Begins

ereign hand in the journey of our lives. With that in mind, let me share some thoughts regarding Job in this opening chapter.

"Have you considered my servant Job?" Whenever I have studied through Job or gone through major trials, I have often thought of this question and wondered how I would react if my name was in that sentence in place of Job's. Would I worship or curse? Would I defend God or defend myself? As we share together in this drama of the life of Job, I would encourage you to keep this question central in your thoughts: What if your name was substituted for Job's and the question was, "Satan, have you considered my servant _____?"

Another thought to consider concerns Job's wife. Oftentimes Job's wife has borne the brunt of a lot of criticism—just or unjust. His wife's words in 2:9, "Still holding on to your precious integrity, are you? Curse God and be done with it!" (The Message), is the advice to her husband to do what Satan predicted he would do—curse God. Of course, she knew that the penalty for cursing God was death. The question is, did she still believe in her husband's faithfulness? Did she really think he would remain righteous under the current circumstances, or had Satan captivated her heart with the doctrine of retribution—great suffering is the result of great sinning? Contrary to many, I lean toward the consideration that she still believed in her husband and loved him to such an extent that she could no longer stand to see him suffer. Consequently, she offers a theological method of ending his suffering—"curse God and die." Unfortunately, we tend to condemn Job's wife in this situation, but in reality, the effect was to increase Job's righteousness. Job withstood immeasurable suffering, so much so that his friends were overwhelmed by his resilience. Of course, Job did have words for his wife, but I tend to think that they weren't as menacing as some translators would have us believe.

Friendly Fire

    At this point we receive one of Job's cornerstone statements: "We take the good days from God, why not the bad ones?" In other words, is it only the people who receive good gifts from God that believe and worship Him? Perhaps Job's response is closer to what Joseph said to his brothers: "As for you, you meant evil against me; but God meant it for good" (Gen. 50:19-20). You may be able to relate to this as well as you consider the evil that has intruded into your life. May God be gracious to us and enable us to respond like Job, "Not once through all this did Job sin. He said nothing against God" (Job 2:10, The Message).

If I sin, what do I do to you, you watcher of mankind? Why have you made me your mark? Why have I become a burden to you?

      Job 7:20

Act II

2

Eliphaz, the Shame-Seller

The Key: Both Job and his friends are hindered in their ability to communicate by their legalistic attitude toward God.

The scene now shifts from Job's interaction with his wife to the outer court of what appears to be a religious meeting place. (The narthex of the First Church of Uz?) As we imagine this scene, we can see three "leadership types," obviously solicitous, planning some action. The dialogue we hear begins with "Say fellows, don't you think Brother Job needs a call?"

>Now when Job's three friends heard of all this evil that had come upon him, they came each from his own place, Eliphaz the

Friendly Fire

> Temanite, Bildad the Shuhite, and Zophar the Naamathite. They made an appointment together to come to show him sympathy and comfort him. (Job 2:11)

Job's bed or pallet would be on the porch of his home, perhaps to take advantage of the healing benefit of the fresh air and sunshine.

> And when they saw him from a distance, they did not recognize him. And they raised their voices and wept, and they tore their robes and sprinkled dust on their heads toward heaven. And they sat with him on the ground seven days and seven nights, and no one spoke a word to him, for they saw that his suffering was very great. (Job 2:12-13)

What can you say to someone who has lost everything? This suffering is too much for words.

This ends the prologue.

THE COLLOQUIES BEGIN[1]

Job's words puzzle and challenge us. Note the wording of the text:

> After this Job opened his mouth and cursed the day of his birth. (Job 3:1)

After what? After his friends had come and wailed and cried aloud with him and shed tears over him. After they sat with him, tore their clothes, sprinkled dust on their heads, and were unable to even speak for seven days and nights. After all that, Job thought, "Surely they are feeling with me enough that I can risk sharing my honest despair."

---

[1] A Colloquy is a synonym for dialogue, used more often when the conversation involves three or more persons; i.e., a conferring of several. (Little, Wm. *The Oxford Universal Dictionary*, 1955).

Eliphaz, the Shame-Seller

But he was wrong, sadly wrong. He must have sensed them recoil, shocked at the intensity of his emotional honesty. Possibly he could have been beaten back right here. Wouldn't most of us? I can put myself in this picture. Three friends have come from church to visit me. I would be tempted to say the things they expected to hear such as, "Thanks for coming, fellows; I know the Lord is good. I'm sure He has something in this for me. I know that all things work together for good; God is on the throne."

They would leave feeling good. They might even make *me* feel good by saying, "Bill, we came to comfort you and you have strengthened us." Sound familiar?

But Job didn't bless them. Rather, he told them exactly what was raging in his soul:

> Let the day perish on which I was born...Let that day be darkness! May God above not seek it...Let it not rejoice among the days of the year; let it not come into the number of the months. [Knock it out of the calendar.] ...Let those curse it who curse the day, who are ready to rouse up Leviathan. [Find a professional day-curser and let the cursing rouse a monster.] (Job 3:3-8)

Job's three friends were not prepared for this. He had said such encouraging words earlier (1:21 and 2:10).

Job now uses the interrogative that comes to the lips of every suffering person:

> Why did I not die at birth?...Why did the knees receive me?...Or why was I not as a hidden stillborn child, as infants who never see the light?...Why is light given to him who is in misery, and life to the bitter in soul, who long for death, but it comes not...Why is light given to a man whose way is hidden, whom God has hedged in? (Job 3:11-23, selected)

Job is so miserable that he wishes he were dead and even that he had never been born. More than that, his suffering is so great that it drives him to ask why God even gives life when such suffering is possible.

In Job's complaint, there are two words the reader should remember. One is the question *"why?,"* the other is "the *hedge.*" The question *"why"* is typical, universally common to sufferers. "The *hedge"* is seen by Satan as a protection for Job, (1:10) but Job sees it as a trap set by an opponent. Be aware that the question *"why"* and the truth of "the *hedge"* will continue throughout the dialogue. Job concludes:

> I am not at ease, nor am I quiet; I have no rest, but trouble comes. (Job 3:26)

It is hard to handle another person's despair. We want to avoid it, or somehow stop the words. It is difficult to know what to say. Too many times I have gone to visit the seriously ill or the tragically bereaved and have cruised around the block several times "trying to find a place to park." When I get to the home or bedside, spiritual sounding clichés come too easily to my mind. They are true, but unfeeling. Better to say little, to reach out and touch, to let them know by your presence that you care.

ELIPHAZ SPEAKS

Eliphaz, who seems to be the leader of the three, feels compelled to answer Job's diatribe. In my imagination (shaped by many years of counseling experience), I hear Eliphaz nervously clear his throat. He would stand over Job. This outburst has been so strong he wants to regain an upper-hand position. Sitting down, eye to eye with Job, would not serve his need to be the authority, the teacher. He tries to appear thoughtful and concerned for Job's feelings, but his question betrays that he expects that Job will resent his judgmental corrections:

Eliphaz, the Shame-Seller

> If one ventures a word with you, will you be impatient? Yet who can keep from speaking? Behold, you have instructed many, and you have strengthened the weak hands. Your words have upheld him who was stumbling, and you have made firm the feeble knees. But now it has come to you, and you are impatient; it touches you, and you are dismayed. (Job 4:2-5)

Now a question—a manipulating, rhetorical question:

> Is not your fear of God your confidence, and the integrity of your ways your hope? Remember: who that was innocent ever perished? Or where were the upright cut off? As I have seen, those who plow iniquity and sow trouble reap the same. By the breath of God they perish, and by the blast of his anger they are consumed. (Job 4:6-9)

He is declaring, "God is angry with evil people and He destroys them, but the innocent are spared." Is Eliphaz intimating that there is something evil in Job?

COLLOQUY ON LEGALISM

If we were watching this drama unfold on a DVD player, I would press the "pause" button right here. We would stop and make some observations that just might be missed. We would get some insight into Eliphaz's thinking. Note, first of all, that the basic premise of his philosophy is that people get what they deserve. Good is rewarded; evil gets punished. Good guys win; bad guys lose. As we continue in our study, we will note that his two friends also have this mind-set.

Eliphaz exposed this thinking when he asked his rhetorical question. Every false expression of religion known to man has its confidence and hope in some kind of pious performance. This thinking is called "legalism." Sometimes it is blatant; sometimes it is subtle. However, the bottom line is that if you keep the rules, laws, shoulds, oughts and taboos, then the "gods" will accept

Friendly Fire

and bless you. Breaking these codes invites rejection and punishment.

The primitive Indian in the jungles of Peru puts three sticks in the river and bows. He hopes the "god of sticks and rivers" will be pleased. The sincere advocates of more sophisticated religious systems get no closer to God by "doing their best" to meet the requirements (implied or stated) of their religion. The basic tenet of this thinking is that confidence before God and rewards from God result from "the integrity of your ways" (4:6). This thinking seeks an acceptance by God based on one's performance. It is a *false hope*.

> He saved us, not because of works done by us in righteousness, but according to his own mercy, by the washing of regeneration and renewal of the Holy Spirit, whom he poured out on us richly through Jesus Christ our Savior, (Titus 3:5-6)

God deals with us today, not on the basis of our "ways," works or behaviors/performance, but on the basis of His grace, appropriated by us through our personal faith in Jesus' death on the cross and His resurrection life and indwelling Spirit. We all deserve death. Grace is God giving these things:

Jesus' righteousness to us,

> For our sake he made him to be sin who knew no sin, so that in him we might become the righteousness of God. (2 Corinthians 5:21)

Jesus' salvation,

> For by grace you have been saved through faith. And this is not your own doing; it is the gift of God, not a result of works, so that no one may boast. (Ephesians 2:8-9)

Jesus' very life into our lives,

> I have been crucified with Christ. It is no longer I who live, but Christ who lives in me. And the life I now live in the flesh I live by

faith in the Son of God, who loved me and gave himself for me. (Galatians 2:20)

GOD'S GRACE IS FREELY GIVEN

All this is given *freely*. All of the doing, working and trying for salvation that can be done has been accomplished for us by Jesus. That is *grace*.

While we are at "pause" in our drama, we make a second observation: an insight into the problem with Eliphaz's thinking when he says to Job, "Shouldn't your trust in God and your blameless ways be your confidence?"

How is Job supposed to feel?

Guilty, that's how.

If I can make a person feel guilty and add a little fear to the guilt, I can control him. All of us have had experience with this ploy. Some of us pastors are professional manipulators by using the accusing finger over the pulpit shaming by comparisons with more austere persons or societies. Spouses attempt to control each other by guilt-pushing arguments. Parents begin early to threaten and shame children. Children learn quickly and soon begin using it against parents so that by the time we are teenagers, we can be highly effective "guilt pushers." This manipulation works; it talks down.

However, a problem that guilt–pushing manipulators do face when they push guilt is that they might not get compliance, but rather they might make the one they are pushing angry. Even worse, they might get deadening acquiescence that shuts them up, even changes outward behaviors, but does not change the heart.

One of the most satisfying facets of my being a pastor for four decades in the same geographic area is that a number of pastors have given me the privilege of encouraging them. Some have

Friendly Fire

come under severe and sometimes unfair attack from their congregations. "I must be doing something wrong," they say. Not necessarily. Satan will see to it that, wrong or not, there will be battles to fight and win. However, I have observed that some, like Eliphaz, who come down hard on God's people from the pedestal of the pulpit, often get a great deal of opposition. There is a seething anger in the congregation; it is hard to argue with all that "rightness."

Thus, it is hard for Job (and for us) to accept Eliphaz's "preaching." Is he an insensitive clod? What would you do if you were one of Job's friends? He continues on with some significant instruction:

> As for me, I would seek God, and to God would I commit my cause, who does great things and unsearchable, marvelous things without number...he sets on high those who are lowly, and those who mourn are lifted to safety. He frustrates the devices of the crafty, so that their hands achieve no success. He catches the wise in their own craftiness, and the schemes of the wily are brought to a quick end...So the poor have hope, and injustice shuts her mouth. Behold, blessed is the one whom God reproves; therefore despise not the discipline of the Almighty (Job 5:8-17)

(Compare with 1 Corinthians 3:19 and Hebrews 12:5-6.)

Obviously, these are good words. Is Eliphaz wrong? No—but yes. They are right words and good teaching, but they are used for the wrong reason—to shut Job up. What Job wants is to unburden himself, to roar out his pain. (He *thought* he was sharing with men who had felt his pain!)

Eliphaz's Moralizing Continues

Eliphaz, the moralistic sermonizer, continues his "sermon."

> For he wounds, but he binds up; he shatters, but his hands heal. (Job 5:18)

Eliphaz, the Shame-Seller

Eliphaz's assessment of God's dealings is "God blesses good people and blasts bad people. If you do evil, He is going to 'zap' you. If you do right, He'll heal your injuries."

> He will deliver you from six troubles; in seven no evil shall touch you. (Job 5:19)

Eliphaz is not counting out seven calamities as much as pronouncing that God will rescue from them all—provided one is good enough.

> In famine he will redeem you from death, and in war from the power of the sword. You shall be hidden from the lash of the tongue, and shall not fear destruction when it comes. At destruction and famine you shall laugh, and shall not fear the beasts of the earth. For you shall be in league with the stones of the field, and the beasts of the field shall be at peace with you. You shall know that your tent is at peace, and you shall inspect your fold and miss nothing. You shall know also that your offspring shall be many, and your descendants as the grass of the earth. You shall come to your grave in ripe old age, like a sheaf gathered up in its season. (Job 5:20-26)

Whew! Here is promised protection or rescue from famine, war, gossip, earthquake and storm. The stones and the animals of the field will fall into place in order to benefit you. The dogs will not bite; you will be safe from burglars; your children will be many and turn out well. (There is a nasty jab here in light of Job's children's troubles and their deaths.) And, you will not be sick, even when it comes time to die. This is "unreal!" We know that life just does not work out this way for anyone, especially God's people. But Eliphaz ends his tack with his "personal endorsement."

> Behold, this we have searched out; it is true. Hear, and know it for your good. (Job 5:27)

So ends Eliphaz's "preaching."

Friendly Fire

At this point Job has an opportunity to say, "Oh brothers, I'm sorry. I shouldn't have gone off like that. Forgive me; I was wrong. I know you meant well, but I'm just not myself." The three would have brightened, probably hugged Job and each other, and Eliphaz could have gone home pleased with himself that his "ministering" had been so successful. But Job is not compliant. He fights back and the heat of the argument rises.

I like sports. The competition is exciting. Winners—losers. Underdogs winning—the arrogant perennial favorites losing. Part of the drama in the book of Job is this competition between Job and his friends. Their comforting fellowship is turning into a fight. The tension escalates because Job will not back down.

Now we press the "play" button and return to the drama. Job is answering Eliphaz:

> Oh that my vexation were weighed, and all my calamity laid in the balances! For then it would be heavier than the sand of the sea; therefore my words have been rash. (Job 6:2-3)

Colloquy on Communicating

If only there was some way for you brothers to feel the heaviness I am carrying, but there is no way to measure despair.

Now Job accuses God of shooting at him, of making him a target:

> For the arrows of the Almighty are in me; my spirit drinks their poison; the terrors of God are arrayed against me. (Job 6:4)

(Also see 7:20; 16:12-13; 19:11-12.)

Herein lies the sub-title of our book, "God, Why Are You Shooting at Me?" (Hasn't everyone, Christian or not, felt that way at some time?) Job throws the gauntlet down. He has bared his soul, and now, he literally slams them with his feelings:

Eliphaz, the Shame-Seller

Does the wild donkey bray when he has grass, or the ox low over his fodder? (Job 6:5)

Am I crying for nothing?

Oh that I might have my request, and that God would fulfill my hope, that it would please God to crush me, that he would let loose his hand and cut me off! This would be my comfort; I would even exult in pain unsparing, for I have not denied the words of the Holy One. (Job 6:8-10)

Why did Job's friends not feel something for him here? He is expressing himself honestly and is concerned about God's Word. Did his friends not "hear" this? Should it not have pulled at their hearts? Did Job give his friends a chance to respond? The lesson here is that we do not listen well when we are defensive or intent on winning.

The hand signal used to call for a "time-out" in a football game is the raised right hand with face high, fingers extended, and an open left palm on top of the right hand to form a "T". Our three boys grew up with a "football mentality." One time when they were young, a "great injustice" occurred. Looking back, it probably was not too important, but because my poise and patience had worn thin, I was storming about it. They were beginning to storm back, and then things became heated when Steve (who later became a football coach) repeatedly pounded his left palm on the top of his right fingers and called, "time-out." It lightened things up and emotions subsided.

It would be so helpful in an argument if we could stop, call "time-out," and listen to feelings.

Job continues his counter-attack in 6:14-7:21.

Fair Weather Friends

Eliphaz's unfeeling, judgmental rebuking has made him angry. He demands, "What kind of friends are you?"

Friendly Fire

> He who withholds kindness from a friend forsakes the fear of the Almighty. (Job 6:14)

"Fair-weather friends are you! You make me feel guilty so I'll 'guilt-push' right back." Job gets graphic, and I must confess that I'm rooting for him here.

Count on you three? Ha! Do you know what you are like? You men…

> …are treacherous as a torrent-bed, as torrential streams that pass away, which are dark with ice, and where the snow hides itself. When they melt, they disappear; when it is hot, they vanish from their place. (Job 6:15-17)

(You are like nice cool water until the "heat's on;" then you dry up.)

> The caravans turn aside from their course; they go up into the waste and perish. The caravans of Tema look, the travelers of Sheba hope. They are ashamed because they were confident; they come there and are disappointed. (Job 6:18-20)

Thirsty travelers thought it was an oasis, but no, it was only a mirage. That is the way Job felt when they sat with him for seven days and seven nights with their mouths shut—betrayed.

> For you have now become nothing; you see my calamity and are afraid. (Job 6:21)

Ouch! Right here Job is bringing the brethren two strong lessons in the art of comforting communication.

COMFORTING COMMUNICATION

The first lesson: I tend to put forth simplistic answers wrapped in spiritual sounding clichés because the other person's painful situation is shaking the ladder I am standing on. I feel threatened; I am nervous; will I say the wrong thing? If the clichés don't hold

Eliphaz, the Shame-Seller

up, where do I go? When trouble hits me, will *I* make it? I am afraid. When one of my friends or acquaintances meets a severe reversal, I ask, "How is he taking it?" O.K., I hope; then I can feel better. It is disquieting for me if he is disintegrating; inwardly I am afraid that that could be me! Fear backs away from pain. Love (agape) moves *into* a situation in spite of the fear.

The second lesson for counseling or comforting anyone (a troubled friend, a spouse or our child) begins with 6:24-25. Job challenges the three:

> Teach me, and I will be silent; make me understand how I have gone astray. (Job 6:24)

He vividly exposes why Eliphaz's good words are not being received.

> How forceful are right words! (Job 6:25a NKJV)

> How forcible are right words! (Job 6:25a KJV)

Job is admitting that what Eliphaz is saying is right, even strong.

> But what does your arguing prove? (Job 6:25b NKJV)

Over and over I am amazed at the relevance of this ancient writing. Job is angry because they are saying what is *right* and ignoring what is *real.* The modern moralist/sermonizer, like Eliphaz, pretends that what *ought to be, is.*

Job relates exactly the reason the sermonizing was "unreal"; i.e., emotionally dishonest and ineffective. How many times this statement of Job has helped me to "hang in there" with a crushed and/or desperately angry person. It has strengthened me to be a more understanding husband, father, pastor and friend. Job says,

> Do you intend to rebuke *my* words, and the speeches of a desperate one, *which are* as wind? (Job 6:26 NKJV)

Friendly Fire

> The speeches of one who is desperate are as wind. (KJV)

> The words of one in despair belong to the wind. (NASB)

Why are you dealing rationally with an emotional outburst? Why are you hanging me on my *words*?

WORDS SPOKEN IN DESPAIR

How often in anger or despair have we spoken words which we did not literally mean? I remember when a middle-aged couple came into my office with their sixteen–year–old son. They had been fighting as a family. Dad related the awful things "Eddie" had said: "I hate you! I'm outa here! I've got places I can go." Mom sat there wiping her eyes. My heart went out to the boy when Dad concluded, "I told him to go ahead! He's never been any good. Anyway, now we know what he *really* thinks of us."

Wrong! So Wrong! Such a mistake! "The speech of a despairing teen (and parent) is as wind." Don't ever let a relationship break over "windy words." Be real! Don't be an Eliphaz but keep Job's correcting question in your mind. No matter who is speaking, when emotions are out of control and tempers flare, those angry words are not from the true heart.

Job now pleads with his friends, Eliphaz in particular:

> But now, be pleased to look at me, for I will not lie to your face. Please turn; let no injustice be done. Turn now; my vindication is at stake. (Job 6:28-29)

His argument is not against the wisdom of their words but the fact that their arguments do not fit. He pleads, "You want me to say what ought to be said whether or not I really feel that way or not. That strips me of my integrity." Integrity and transparency are at the root of being real. To the end of the drama, Job will fight to maintain his integrity.

Eliphaz, the Shame-Seller

Chapter seven concludes Job's answer to Eliphaz. It is a sobering description of the heartache of the critically ill.

> When I lie down I say, "When shall I arise?" But the night is long, and I am full of tossing till the dawn. My flesh is clothed with worms and dirt; my skin hardens, then breaks out afresh. My days are swifter than a weaver's shuttle and come to their end without hope. Remember that my life is a breath; my eye will never again see good. (Job 7:4-7)

He maintains that since he has nothing more to lose, he will not keep silent or say the "right words" dishonestly. Rather, he says,

> Therefore I will not restrain my mouth; I will speak in the anguish of my spirit; I will complain in the bitterness of my soul...I loathe my life; I would not live forever. Leave me alone, for my days are a breath. What is man, that you make so much of him, and that you set your heart on him, visit him every morning and test him every moment? (Job 7:11,16-18)

JOB'S ANGER TURNS TO GOD

At this point, Job's defense against Eliphaz's moralizing turns to anger against God. Although it saddens us, it is real enough. In 7:17 he asks the question of God that David, in Psalm 8:4, and the writer of the book of Hebrews (2:6) asked in a different spirit. They ask, "God, You are so great and we are so small, why do you even think about us?" Job asks, "Why, when man is so small, are you giving me all this attention? Why are you so relentlessly on my case?" In this terrible pain, he does not understand the reason God has allowed such awful things to happen to him; thus, he demands,

> Have I sinned? What have I done to You, O watcher of men? Why have You set me as Your target, so that I am a burden to myself? (Job 7:20 NKJV)

Friendly Fire

To the student of Scripture, there is an interesting and enlightening translation difference regarding 7:20. Both the KJV and NASB read, "…So that I am a burden to myself." Is not this feeling of alienation from God and from ourselves a significant part of the anguish of suffering? In dark times I have thought, "I don't like myself this way."

As Job's answer to Eliphaz ends, he expresses again strong feelings that God has targeted him and he does not know why.

The perplexing puzzle of "why bad things happen to good people" has troubled humanity from the beginning. In this book, there is at least part of the answer to that "why." It will impact us with power as the drama unfolds and the meaning of the "target" becomes clearer.

Eliphaz has had the satisfaction of giving Job "the Word." He probably thought of himself as quite courageous. (After all, it takes guts to sail into someone who is hurting that much!) But his efforts have failed. Job has been neither comforted nor corrected.

Maybe you have been the sufferer, the wounded one in some situation. The comforters gang up on you. The pressure to agree, to say the right words, to be comforted will escalate. Those who are right, *must* be right.

GROUP STUDY GUIDE AND PERSONAL APPLICATION

1. The purpose for the visit of Job's three friends, Eliphaz, Bildad and Zophar, was to sympathize with him and to comfort him. They hardly recognized Job, for his disease was so disfiguring. In expression of their deep mourning, what three things did the friends do to express their grief?

Eliphaz, the Shame-Seller

2. For a whole week Job and his friends sat in silence. Then, allowing the grieving person to speak first, they listened as Job uttered his first words to the shock of his comforters. What were Job's words in Job 3:1? Why do they shock his listeners? Knowing Job's earlier responses to his plight, are you surprised by this, too? Why?

3. List the things Job said he wished had happened regarding his conception and birth. Ultimately, he was asking why God ever allows humans to be born if only to experience great suffering. When a friend of yours is suffering greatly, do you long to be with him or do you shy away from him? Why?

4. Eliphaz, though appearing to be concerned for Job's feelings, insinuates that Job himself is the cause of his own trouble. State Eliphaz's philosophy about the reason bad things happen to people.

5. Titus 3:5-6 refutes the thinking that our acceptance before God is based on our performance. Write these verses in your own words. On what basis does God deal with people today?

6. Can a person ever be good enough to merit Christ's salvation? How does man come into a right relationship to God according to Ephesians 2:8-9? If we *could* be saved by our own good works, what would we be tempted to do?

7. Using a dictionary, define the word *grace*. How does your definition apply to what Jesus has done for you?

8. At times people use guilt in an attempt to motivate others. What did Eliphaz say to Job in an attempt to make Job feel guilty for supposed wrongdoing? Can you remember a time when you tried to motivate someone to change his behavior by making him feel guilty? ("You're not going to have *another* piece of cake, are you?") How did that person respond to you?

Friendly Fire

9. Eliphaz finished his preaching about the way in which God rescues righteous people by adding that he and his friends have examined his sermon and declared it to be truth. Job need only apply it to his life. Job, however, intended to hold to his position. He knew that he had not sinned, and he turned his accusations toward God. What was Job expressing to God?

10. Job had one consolation and joy in the midst of his extreme suffering. What was it?

11. Why do you suppose Job's friends did not seem to listen to him when he claimed that he had not denied God's words? Have you ever found yourself to be hearing only what you wanted to hear?

12. Job is clearly disappointed in his friends. How does he describe them? What does he say to them about their "help"?

13. Fear backs away from pain. Love (Agape) moves into a situation in spite of the fear. Think of a time when you failed to "be there" for a friend because you were afraid of what to say. How could you have handled the situation more lovingly?

14. Eliphaz was saying some right words, but Job asked, "What do your right words prove?" Rather than "telling it like it is" (from Eliphaz's perspective), what would have been a better approach in dealing with Job? At times we all say words hastily and emotionally which we do not mean literally. Write in your own words Job's correcting question (Job 6:26).

15. When he feels he has no more to lose, that he will never be happy again, Job turns his anger toward God. What questions is he asking God? To what question does Job demand an answer from God? Does he get an answer? Why do you think God chose not to answer?

16. Have you ever questioned God about the way in which He was dealing with you? What have you seen in retrospect that you could not see at the time you faced your struggle?

Don's Reflections

As Pastor Bill leads us into chapter two there is almost the feeling that Job's three friends were members of the same church—The First Church of Uz. In reality, these three lived some distance apart—250-300 miles. It doesn't change the essence of the drama, but it does give us a better handle on the extent of time involved in Job's travail. For information to get to these men regarding Job and then communicate back to each other that they should visit their friend, probably took weeks if not months. There is no indication in Scripture as to the amount of time between the onset of Job's travail and the arrival of his friends, but his physical appearance had evidently shown the toll of his illness because "...when they first caught sight of him, they couldn't believe what they saw—they hardly recognized him!" (The Message). They cried out and wept, and they observed the rituals of mourning and silently sat with him on the ash heap for seven days and seven nights, the traditional period of mourning for the dead (Gen. 50:10; 1 Sam. 31:13).

Wouldn't it be easy (maybe even fun) to jump on these three friends and criticize their "comforting" words? But, before we become too critical, someone has pointed out that several things can be said in their favor: (a) they came to visit Job when he was ill; (b) they sat with him in silence for seven days and seven nights while he suffered greatly; and (c) when they had something to say they did not go behind his back. They were upfront and spoke to him face to face. They had the courage of their convictions.

Friendly Fire

Unfortunately, Job's friends failed in the very thing they came to do—counsel and comfort. Counseling today is significant. Ironically, George Adam Smith, a noted 19th century commentator and author, said, "The speeches of Job's friends ought to be studied by every man who proposes to make the guidance and consolation of his fellow-man in their religious interests, the duty of his life."[2] Please note the date of this publication—this advice was offered in 1901!

Some years ago we were reeling from a not-so-pleasant church planting experience. We were in need of comfort and grace-filled counsel but received much of the "Eliphaz theology." One pastor even commented, "You failed, face it and move on!" We could certainly relate to the "arrows of the Almighty..." (6:4). It literally took years to recover as we asked, "...why have You set us as Your target?" (7:20 NASB).

As believers we often find ourselves in positions where counsel may be asked of us. Prayerfully consider what God would have you offer. "For the despairing man there should be kindness from his friends..." (6:14).

---

[2] George Adam Smith, *Modern Criticism and the Old Testament*, (New York: A.C. Armstrong and Son, 1901), p. 298.

After the LORD had spoken these words to Job, the LORD said to Eliphaz the Temanite: "My anger burns against you and against your two friends, for you have not spoken of me what is right, as my servant Job has."

Job 42:7

3

Bildad, the Oversimplifier

The Key: Jesus does not give us a list of behaviors to perform or a catalog of answers to our questions; rather, He gives us Himself.

The scene changes. The spotlight moves to Job and the second friend.

Before we get into Bildad's speech, think with me about the kind of relationship Job has with God. We might quickly judge it as "poor." However, if we do, we are in trouble. *We* know something that neither Job nor his friends knew. God Himself declared Job to be blameless and upright (1:1). Satan is permitted by God to ravish him *"without reason"* (2:3). Job complains with honesty. He pours out his bad thoughts and feelings to his

Friendly Fire

friends and to God, but his friends cannot take the honesty. But can God take honesty? The prophet Ezekiel lists Job as a hero along with Noah and Daniel (Ezekiel 14:14,20), and the Apostle James notes that he is a good example of one who persevered in waiting on God (James 5:10-11).

Job's emotional honesty and vulnerability make a dramatic, Scripture-based statement that *it is more important to God that we be real than that we appear right.*

The Lord said to Eliphaz...

> ...the LORD said to Eliphaz the Temanite: "My anger burns against you and against your two friends, for you have not spoken of me what is right, as my servant Job has." (Job 42:7)

COLLOQUY ON MANIPULATION VS. MOTIVATION

As Bildad begins to speak, the emotional temperature rises a few degrees.

> How long will you say these things, and the words of your mouth be a great wind? (Job 8:2)

Apparently Job's discourse on dealing with emotional outbursts got under Bildad's skin, so he asks,

> Does God pervert justice? Or does the Almighty pervert the right? (Job 8:3)

This is a rhetorical question; Bildad does not seek an answer for both he and Job know the answer. His purpose is to shame, intimidate and manipulate. Like Eliphaz, Bildad counts on guilt and fear to beat Job back and to shut him up. He follows with a low blow.

> If your children have sinned against him, he has delivered them into the hand of their transgression. (Job 8:4)

Bildad, the Oversimplifier

In Bildad's thinking, since Job's wayward children were blown away by God, they got what they deserved. He is implying that Job is probably getting what he deserved, too. This is a primitive idea; we are all acquainted with it. Someone whose testimony in Christian service was notable walks into a life of flagrant and deliberate disobedience. Trouble hits him. We think, "No wonder! What can you expect?" If *we* enter a season of trouble we say, "Lord, what am I doing wrong?" It may be an ancient idea, but it is also modern.

GUILT AND GRACE

Some years ago when I was a speaker at a retreat for missionaries, a young man came to question me. He was courteous, but I could tell he was upset. "What is so terrible about guilt? Sin is sin. Why be so careful about making people feel guilty? Isn't this just a way of treating sin lightly? Can't guilt drive us to grace?"

When Nathan the prophet dealt with King David about his adultery with Bathsheba and the murder of Uriah (2 Samuel 12), he told David a parable about two men in a certain town—one was rich, the other was poor. The rich man had many sheep and lambs; the poor man had only one ewe lamb. A traveler came to the rich man's house and, instead of taking one of his own lambs, he took the poor man's and served it for dinner. David was incensed; "This man deserves to die. He must pay for his lack of pity." "You are the man, David," said Nathan. "You have despised the word of the Lord." David's response was, "I have sinned."

Nathan's words exploded in David's mind like a bomb. In the 51st Psalm, he pours out his confession and expresses his repentance. He spends the rest of his life working through the bitter consequences.

Nathan had come to David in the spirit of Galatians six.

> Brothers, if anyone is caught in any transgression, you who are spiritual should restore him in a spirit of gentleness. Keep watch

> on yourself, lest you too be tempted. Bear one another's burdens, and so fulfill the law of Christ. (Galatians 6:1-2)

This confrontation brought David to repentance. Actual, perceived guilt drove him to grace and deliverance. Obviously, real guilt must be dealt with, and it can be. There is no limit to God's grace towards His sinning child:

> In him we have redemption through his blood, the forgiveness of our trespasses, according to the riches of his grace, which he lavished upon us, in all wisdom and insight (Ephesians 1:7-8)

However, threatening, shaming and frightening in order to manipulate and pressure someone into compliance with a certain way of behaving or thinking is not only cruel and useless, but ***wrong***.

> After the LORD had spoken these words to Job, the LORD said to Eliphaz the Temanite: "My anger burns against you and against your two friends, for you have not spoken of me what is right, as my servant Job has. Now therefore take seven bulls and seven rams and go to my servant Job and offer up a burnt offering for yourselves. And my servant Job shall pray for you, for I will accept his prayer not to deal with you according to your folly. For you have not spoken of me what is right, as my servant Job has." (Job 42:7-8)

Humility and Help for the Hurting

It takes genuine humility to help an erring, hurting person. It is easy to "practice our religion" on others. When we do this, we are serving ourselves and our own thinking instead of having a heart for them. This is what "spiritual abuse" looks like. It looks like Eliphaz and Bildad, and unfortunately, it looks like too many of the rest of us also.

Through the years, many spiritually abused people have sought out the Moraine Valley Church, my home church, in

Bildad, the Oversimplifier

Palos Heights, Illinois. In counseling situations, we would hear, "Moraine is a healing place. We came here all beat up; now we are getting stronger. We are finally able to trust enough to be vulnerable again." As we talked, they realized that, rather than being manipulated into Christian living by guilt and fear, they were being motivated by grace and love.

Bildad continues with an easy solution to Job's problem—a formula for "what to do to make everything all right."

"But if you will
  I. Look to God.
  II. Plead with the Almighty (Pray).
  III. Be pure and upright.
  IV. Then, presto! Even now He will rouse Himself on your behalf and restore you to your rightful place."

> If you will seek God and plead with the Almighty for mercy, if you are pure and upright, surely then he will rouse himself for you and restore your rightful habitation. (Job 8:5-6)

> He will fix your situation so well and your future will be so prosperous, that what you had in the beginning will seem downright humble! If you straighten up, Job, your mouth will be filled with laughter, you will shout for joy. Just take this "antidote," follow the formula and have faith. (Job 8:7,20-21, paraphrased.)

COLLOQUY ON SPIRITUAL TECHNOLOGY

Whereas Eliphaz was a "sermonizer," talking down to Job, Bildad continues with simplistic answers. He gives him something to *do,* some steps to take. He has a formula—a spiritual "technology." Just master the mechanics and the directions of what to do, and your problems will be solved.

The problem with Bildad's counseling is oversimplification; "the good *always* prosper and the bad *always* suffer." Such

Friendly Fire

thinking does not consider all the facts; it plays God. *Not having the problem, Bildad has the answers.*

As we have observed the behavior of a relative's or friend's child, have we not said, "If I had that kid, etc." Not having him, you know exactly what the problem is and what disciplines should be applied to correct it. If the problem is marriage or handling money or raising children or one's own Christian behavior and character, we want to think it could be corrected if we could just get the right instructions or follow the right formula. Many teachers, counselors and seminar leaders hold out the promise that their "system" will work.

We modern Americans idolize "technology." We focus on getting the right information. We think, "I'm going to work hard at what this new book tells me. I'm going to put into practice the insights and steps that the seminar leader points out. I'll work at making this formula effective in my life."

It is not that the formula is faulty but that we are counting on *what we can do* to make a change. We just *have* to get it right. The truth is, IT never works; HE, God works.

The living presence of Christ in us must be central to our hope. It is not what we do, it is what Jesus does; His life and power in us works.

> work out your own salvation with fear and trembling, for it is God who works in you, both to will and to work for his good pleasure. (Philippians 2:12b-13)

Focus on Jesus, alive in you. Quit struggling and believe Him. Recognize that He is in you to develop a conscious, personal fellowship with you. When we stop looking to some strength in ourselves, Jesus gently makes changes.

> I am the vine; you are the branches. Whoever abides in me and I in him, he it is that bears much fruit, for apart from me you can do nothing. (John 15:5)

Bildad, the Oversimplifier

One of my greatest joys in being a child of God is my experience of Jesus doing in me things I know I could not accomplish by my own will power or *trying,* struggling, even praying for help. Habits, besetting sins, destructive behaviors and thinking are chains that bind me. I almost despair of ever being loosed. Then, I see that Christ is in me for *this*!

Charles Wesley's hymn expresses my heart response:

> Long my imprisoned spirit lay
> Fast bound in sin and nature's night;
> Thine eye diffused a quick'ning ray,
> I woke, the dungeon flamed with light;
> My chains fell off, my heart was free;
> I rose, went forth, and followed thee.

And worship flows in me and out of me as I sing

> Amazing Love! How can it be that
> Thou, my God, shouldst die for me![3]

JOB ANSWERS BILDAD

Job now attempts to answer Bildad's over-simplifications. He agrees, in part.

> Then Job answered and said: "Truly I know that it is so: But how can a man be in the right before God? If one wished to contend with him, one could not answer him once in a thousand times." (Job 9:1-3)

Job lived 2,000 years before Jesus. Obviously, he did not know Him, but he knew God in the way those ancient people—Abraham, Isaac, Jacob and Joseph—knew Him.

Job continues.

---

[3]Charles Wesley, (1708-1788), *And Can It Be That I Should Gain?*

Friendly Fire

> He is wise in heart and mighty in strength—who has hardened himself against him, and succeeded?—he who removes mountains, and they know it not, when he overturns them in his anger, who shakes the earth out of its place, and its pillars tremble; who commands the sun, and it does not rise; who seals up the stars; who alone stretched out the heavens and trampled the waves of the sea; who made the Bear and Orion, the Pleiades and the chambers of the south; who does great things beyond searching out, and marvelous things beyond number…Who will say to him, "What are you doing?" (Job 9:4-10,12b)

Job believes all this; it is how he *thinks*. But he knows that even if he wished to dispute with Him, he could not answer God but only plead with Him for mercy. He says,

> If I summoned him and he answered me, I would not believe that he was listening to my voice. (Job 9:16)

(What if I called, "God, come here; I want to talk with you." What if He came? I would not have a chance!)

> For he crushes me with a tempest and multiplies my wounds without cause; he will not let me get my breath, but fills me with bitterness. (Job 9:17-18)

(Like one coming up for air, He would keep pushing me down under…)

> If it is a contest of strength, behold, he is mighty! If it is a matter of justice, who can summon him? Though I am in the right, my own mouth would condemn me; though I am blameless, he would prove me perverse. (Job 9:19-20)

(How could I win?)

> It is all one; therefore I say, He destroys both the blameless and the wicked…if it is not he, who then is it? (Job 9:22,24b)

Bildad, the Oversimplifier

God's ways are hard for us to fathom. There is something about Job's turmoil that stings us with doubt.

As a young pastor in the years just after World War II, I was visiting in a trailer park in Stone Park, Illinois. I knocked on the door of a trailer and a burly fellow opened it with, "Yeaah, whadaya want?" I stammered, "I'm the pastor of the Melrose Park Bible Church and I want to…" "Listen you," he pulled me inside, "I don't hate you, but I sure don't like your God. I was in the regiment that released the prisoners in the German death camps. I saw real evil. If there is a God and He let that happen, then He is either weak or He doesn't care! Either way, I don't need Him." I did not have a ready answer, but it probably would have made no difference. With a quick shove, I was immediately outside of the trailer looking at the closed door. This *is* a tough question, and it is the way Job feels.

COLLOQUY ON THE MEDIATOR AND JESUS BEING "REAL"

I do not think that Job would have responded well to "possibility thinking" or to a "positive mental attitude" teaching at this point. Talking to his friends, he says,

> If I say, "I will forget my complaint, I will put off my sad face, and be of good cheer," I become afraid of all my suffering, for I know you will not hold me innocent. I shall be condemned; why then do I labor in vain? If I wash myself with snow and cleanse my hands with lye, yet you will plunge me into a pit, and my own clothes will abhor me." (Job 9:27-31)

Job talks about God again,

> For he is not a man, as I am, that I might answer him, that we should come to trial together. There is no arbiter between us, who might lay his hand on us both. (Job 9:32-33)

Friendly Fire

(One translation of "one to arbitrate" is *daysman*, another is *mediator*.)

> Let him take his rod away from me, and let not dread of him terrify me. Then I would speak without fear of him, for I am not so in myself. (Job 9:34-35)

Job longs for someone who will say, "I have my hand on God, Job, and I have my hand on you. And because I am who I am, I can bring you together."

Although Job could not see that One, we do; His name is Jesus.

> For there is one God, and there is one mediator between God and men, the man Christ Jesus, (1 Timothy 2:5)

He is that One Job longed for. For you and me, *that longed for one is here, now.* If you are hurting as you read this, I will not give you a sermon, a formula, nor a plan to correct your ways. I will point you to Jesus, to the One who is saying to you,

> Come to me, all who labor and are heavy laden, and I will give you rest. (Matthew 11:28)

Jesus does not give answers to all our questions; He gives us Himself.

Job's three friends, as well as present day comforters, are often sure that the simple offer of themselves is not enough. They have to give something, even if it is only advice.

Jesus is Sufficient

My wife and I stood in line at the funeral home. A young Air Force pilot had been killed in a training accident. He was a flight instructor, a graduate with highest honors from the Air Force Academy. As a church family we were proud of him. His mom taught one of our ladies' Bible classes; his dad served as a dea-

Bildad, the Oversimplifier

con. We were all shocked and grief-stricken. As the line moved forward, I watched the family display poise in their grief, yet naturally shed tears from time to time. I heard the woman in front of us, in a voice "dripping" with concern, approach the family and say, "I just know that this will cause many of our young people to examine their lives. Young people are so confident they can't be taken. We know all things work together for good; God is on the throne; He doesn't make mistakes. I'm sure many will be saved through David's tragic death." His mother visibly paled as she spoke, then the woman moved along to share her insights with others.

I cringed inside. As Pastor, I felt restrained from piling on more *words,* so I just stood there, misty-eyed and held their hands, then moved on. A few days later, I received a note, "Thank you, Pastor, for feeling with me. *He* is enough."

Is Jesus "real" to you in this way? Before leaving His disciples, Jesus instructed them and us,

> In that day [the day the Holy Spirit comes into a life] you will know that I am in my Father, and you in me, and I in you. (John 14:20)

Such intimacy! The Apostle Paul, writing to the Colossians, also affirms the same truth:

> of which I became a minister according to the stewardship from God that was given to me for you, to make the word of God fully known, the mystery hidden for ages and generations but now revealed to his saints. To them God chose to make known how great among the Gentiles are the riches of the glory of this mystery, which is Christ in you, the hope of glory. [Living gloriously now, not glory, "bye and bye."] (Colossians 1:25-27)

Many of us may shrug our shoulders at this point. We agree that it *is* sound Bible doctrine, but experiencing intimacy with Jesus seems beyond us. The legalistic approach of Job's three

Friendly Fire

friends addressed only external behaviors. Job wanted more; he *believed* there was more; he longed for a personal encounter. Because the Holy Spirit had not yet come to live in believers, such intimacy was beyond Job.

However, it is not beyond us. We are living on "the light" side of Calvary. Jesus died and rose from the dead. He is alive now and has sent the Holy Spirit into the world to live in those who have received Him. Jesus promised this intimacy when He taught in the temple.

> On the last day of the feast, the great day, Jesus stood up and cried out, "If anyone thirsts, let him come to me and drink. Whoever believes in me, as the Scripture has said, 'Out of his heart will flow rivers of living water.'" Now this he said about the Spirit, whom those who believed in him were to receive, for as yet the Spirit had not been given, because Jesus was not yet glorified. (John 7:37-39)

Jesus invites us into intimacy when He says,

> Come to me, all who labor and are heavy laden, and I will give you rest. Take my yoke upon you, and learn from me, for I am gentle and lowly in heart, and you will find rest for your souls. For my yoke is easy, and my burden is light. (Matthew 11:28-30)

SEEKING INTIMACY

In my early years of pastoring, I became acquainted with The Navigators organization. Through Jack Mayhall, one of their staff members, God opened my life to the dynamic of discipling "man to man." The basis for this work is Paul's instruction to his young pastoral protégé, Timothy:

> You then, my child, be strengthened by the grace that is in Christ Jesus, and what you have heard from me in the presence of many witnesses entrust to faithful men who will be able to teach others also. (2 Timothy 2:1-2)

Bildad, the Oversimplifier

One of the choicest "reliable men" that God sent to me was Len, a recent graduate in business who was beginning his career. We met early each Tuesday morning and memorized Scripture, using The Navigator's Topical Memory System, of course. We did Bible studies and discussed basic aspects of becoming established in a walk with God. One morning soon after we had begun, Len recited,

> Whoever has my commandments and keeps them, he it is who loves me. And he who loves me will be loved by my Father, and I will love him and manifest myself to him. (John 14:21)

"Pastor, I don't get that; Jesus hasn't 'manifested' (KJV) Himself to me. What does that mean? Is it that Jesus isn't 'real' to me?" I was chagrined that I didn't have a ready answer. I rather quickly thought on the "commandment" requirement, and asked him, "Is there some area of disobedience?"

Len replied thoughtfully, "Pastor, I'm not perfect, but I don't know of any...maybe...well, I just don't know." I wondered, "Why am *I* struggling so with this?" I glanced at my watch, hoping the time was up. Two minutes to go. "Let's begin here next week, Len, O.K.?" "Whew," I thought to myself, "I didn't do that well, but I'll have time to look up a better answer for next week."

During that week God did lead to another verse:

> And without faith it is impossible to please him, for whoever would draw near to God must believe that he exists and that he rewards those who seek him. (Hebrews 11:6)

The two phrases, *"believe that He exists"* and believe *"that he rewards those who earnestly seek him"* stood out in my mind in bold relief. I'll never forget the following Tuesday morning. There were no spiritual sky-rockets, just Len's saying, "Pastor, I think I'm getting it." A friend of his had given him the Hebrews eleven

Friendly Fire

verse. I had mulled those verses for a week. It became apparent to both of us that these Scriptures had caused us to see the difference in the "religion" part of our faith and the personal fellowship with Jesus. Believing that Jesus *did* exist in an objective, impersonal way is different from believing that He is alive in me *now*. Len acknowledged that he possibly had had secret doubts about Jesus being real in his own heart.

Jesus being real. As a pastor, sure, I had experienced times of blessing, joy and love for Jesus but my stumbling with answers for Len had forced me to look at the hard question, "Was Jesus *real* to me?" Could it be that the church, Bible study, preaching, status, the work of the ministry, fellowship with Christian friends, the "strokes" that come from the congregation—all of these externals—were more "real" to me than the Jesus who lived in me? I began to recognize intimacy and to seek it earnestly. Helping Len with his honest question helped me to grow. Truly, "As iron sharpens iron, so one person sharpens the life of his or her friend" (Proverbs 27:17, paraphrased).

Now, back to the drama and the dialogue. Because Job's eloquent longing for a mediator (9:33) has no effect on his visitors, he gives full vent to his feelings. His accusations against God embarrass us:

> I loathe my life; I will give free utterance to my complaint; I will speak in the bitterness of my soul...Does it seem good to you to oppress, to despise the work of your hands and favor the designs of the wicked?...And were my head lifted up, you would hunt me like a lion and again work wonders against me...Why did you bring me out from the womb? Would that I had died before any eye had seen me. (Job 10:1,3,16,18)

It is this cry of despair that brings Zophar into the fray.

Bildad, the Oversimplifier

GROUP STUDY GUIDE
AND PERSONAL APPLICATION

1. Though Job poured out his bad feelings to God and to his friends, still he did it with emotional honesty. What does Job 42:7 tell us about the way in which God viewed Job's honesty? What did God have to say about the honesty of Job's friends?

2. Bildad implied that Job and his children received what they deserved. Why is Job 8:4 an especially low blow to Job? (Refer to Job 1:5.)

3. Discuss the differences between confrontation of actual sin leading to repentance and manipulation of another person in order to get him to comply with a certain behavior.

4. How should we help a person who we know is continuing in sin? According to Ephesians 1:7-8 what does God do for us when we confess our sin?

5. Summarize Bildad's solution to Job's suffering. What is wrong with his counsel?

6. It is easy to come up with quick, simplistic solutions to problems, determining that by following a certain system we can affect change. What does this philosophy forget? What should our focus be according to Philippians 2:12-13?

7. Jesus works in the lives of His children. In John 15:5 how does God describe Himself and His children? What does He tell us to do? What does it mean to remain *in Him*?

8. Job knows how great and awesome God is, and He does not dispute that fact. It is God's actions which he questions. Do you ever feel that you just cannot win in dealing with God? Are you able to express honestly to Him the way in which you feel?

Friendly Fire

9. Job has a wish as expressed in Job 9:32-33. What is it? Though Job did not know it, for whom was he actually asking? What can Jesus do for us which no one else can do?

10. Job did not have the Scriptures as we do. He could not understand the mystery of "Christ in you, the hope of glory." How do people today experience true intimacy with Christ?

11. Jesus invites people to come to Him. How does His description of Himself in Matthew 11:28-30 contrast with Job's view of God in Job 9:16-18 and 10:18?

12. Read Hebrews 11:6. What two things must a person who comes to God believe? Why is it important that we do more than just believe that Jesus existed? Do you earnestly seek intimacy with Him?

Don's Reflections

As Pastor Bill so aptly points out in this chapter, Bildad is the consummate "oversimplifier." He had all the answers and even a 1-2-3 formula without ever experiencing the pain.

Our present Senior Pastor at Moraine Valley Church, Pastor Pat Peglow, in one of his sermons commented that "God uses pain to change us." Pastor Pat's sermon came from 1 Samuel 2 and 3 where God deals with Eli and his sons. God chastises Eli severely, and Eli experiences the premature death of his two sons. Eli's punishment was "...for the iniquity that he knew, 'because his sons were blaspheming God, and he did not restrain them'" (1 Sam. 3:13).

As I listened, I could not help but think of Job who, some 500 years earlier, was so concerned about the spiritual welfare of his children. His concern was so intense that one commentator states, "To ensure the innocent standing of his children had been Job's most urgent duty, according to the prologue (1:5), since he

Bildad, the Oversimplifier

himself had always feared that they might have 'sinned in their hearts,' and had 'continually' offered sacrifices to decontaminate them from sin." The commentator goes on to say, "There is no reason in the narrative to suppose that the fate of Job's sons and daughters was the result of their behavior; for Job, his children's fate and his own are equally inexplicable."[4]

But, the "counselors" continued to hammer at Job with their theology of retribution—God blesses the good and punishes the bad. Having four married children and twenty grandchildren, my wife and I have been extremely blessed. When Bildad, without pity, slams Job by using the example of Job's children to defend his theology, I cringed as most surely many of you whom God has privileged to raise children must be doing at Bildad's guilt-pushing speech.

In the mix of our children we have two sons, and as you may have deduced, two sons-in-law (we have never considered them "in-laws" as such but love them dearly and consider each of them as one of our "four" sons). Two are serving God as pastors, and two are serving God in other vocations.

Ironically (??)—or, as God would have it in His sovereign plan—each has experienced life threatening illnesses or accidents. As parents, God has allowed us to persevere through each situation, and I believe our walk with Him has been enriched. But, as a parent, in each situation, I found myself asking (crying out), "Lord what have I done? What is there in my life that has allowed this to happen to _my_ children?" In each situation God has had to remind me that these are _His_ children whom He has loaned to us for a time, and He _will_ bring glory to His name in whatever outcome He should choose! He has! They are! We have grown!

---

[4] *Word Biblical Commentary*, (Dallas, TX: Word Books, Vol. 17, 1989), p. 203.

Behold, my eye has seen all this, my ear has heard and understood it. What you know, I also know; I am not inferior to you. But I would speak to the Almighty, and I desire to argue my case with God.

        Job 13:1-3

4

Zophar, the Zealot

The Key: How weak are our attempts to "help" God or defend His ways. We are false witnesses when we pretend that what ought to be, is.

Zophar is not the brightest of the three. Like many bigots, he was short on intelligence and long on emotion. In fact, he does not have anything to add to the dialogue except his "guilt bombs"—harsh and blunt—and bound into the same mind-set as his companions in comfort. He scolds,

> Should your babble silence men, and when you mock, shall no one shame you? (Job 11:3)

Isn't it odd that they came to *"comfort?"* With no feeling and very little thought, Zophar pounds away:

Friendly Fire

Know then that God exacts of you less than your guilt deserves. (Job 11:6b)

(You are better off than you deserve.)

For he knows worthless men; when he sees iniquity, will he not consider it? But a stupid man will get understanding when a wild donkey's colt is born a man! (Job 11:11-12)

(Unless you quickly agree with us, you will prove that you are an idiot. But your type does not change any more than a wild ass's colt can be born a man. If you want to be thought a jackass, so be it!)

That is the way you are, Job. Case closed. In Zophar's mind, Job is put in a box stamped "inferior, rejected, judged," and the box is nailed shut. Zophar is judgmental to the core.

Now, Zophar has a *sermon*; all Job has to do is

<u>Make a commitment</u>

If you prepare your heart, (Job 11:13a)

<u>Pray</u>

you will stretch out your hands toward him. (Job 11:13b)

<u>Live a "separated" life</u>

If iniquity is in your hand, put it far away, and let not injustice dwell in your tents. (Job 11:14)

<u>Then, results are assured</u>

Surely then you will lift up your face without blemish; you will be secure and will not fear. You will forget your misery; you will remember it as waters that have passed away. And your life will be brighter than the noonday; its darkness will be like the morning. And you will feel secure, because there is hope; you will look around and take your rest in security. (Job 11:15-18)

Zophar, the Zealot

I have difficulty liking people such as Zophar. Eliphaz was a shame-seller, a sermonizer; Bildad was an over-simplifier; but Zophar is plainly a bigot (*"Da Judge"*). What seems right to him, is right, period. Not only that, he is a bully.

I am amazed at Job's resilience. After being pounded by Zophar, he comes back with a smashing counterattack:

> No doubt you are the people, and wisdom will die with you. But I have understanding as well as you; I am not inferior to you. Who does not know such things as these? (Job 12:2-3)

(Do not talk down to me.)

As a seminary student, I would engage my mother (a Bible teacher for many years in the Chicago area) in my newly learned approaches to theological controversies. I get an echo in my mind of these words of Job, "Bill, wisdom will die with you."

Job adds,

> In the thought of one who is at ease there is contempt for misfortune; it is ready for those whose feet slip. (Job 12:5)

Job's inner honesty enables him to sense something in his friends that many of us may recognize. Have you ever received news of the misfortune of a rich friend or relative and felt some shock and dismay, but not totally? Something down deep is pleased? Job is feeling this from the three, and it makes him angry.

COLLOQUY ON LYING FOR GOD

Job now counters their claim that the wicked always suffer and fail.

> The tents of robbers are at peace, and those who provoke God are secure, who bring their god in their hand. (Job 12:6)

(What a description of the materialist of any time period, the worshiper of things.)

Friendly Fire

Job eloquently contends that bad people often prosper.

> But ask the beasts, and they will teach you; the birds of the heavens, and they will tell you; or the bushes of the earth, and they will teach you; and the fish of the sea will declare to you. Who among all these does not know that the hand of the LORD has done this? In his hand is the life of every living thing and the breath of all mankind. (Job 12:7-10)

We inwardly cringe as he runs through a catalogue of bad things that come to good people. He insists it is the hand of God that controls these happenings, and he is angry about it.

> He leads counselors away stripped, and judges he makes fools. He looses the bonds of kings and binds a waistcloth on their hips. He leads priests away stripped and overthrows the mighty. He deprives of speech those who are trusted and takes away the discernment of the elders. He pours contempt on princes and loosens the belt of the strong. He uncovers the deeps out of darkness and brings deep darkness to light. He makes nations great, and he destroys them; he enlarges nations, and leads them away. He takes away understanding from the chiefs of the people of the earth and makes them wander in a pathless waste. They grope in the dark without light, and he makes them stagger like a drunken man. (Job 12:17-25)

Probably emboldened by his own eloquence, Job turns up the heat.

> Behold, my eye has seen all this, my ear has heard and understood it. What you know, I also know; I am not inferior to you. But I would speak to the Almighty, and I desire to argue my case with God. (Job 13:1-3)

(I am tired of arguing with you; I want to talk to God.)

> As for you, you whitewash with lies; worthless physicians are you all. (Job 13:4)

Zophar, the Zealot

The New King James Version translates, *"But you forgers of lies."* The New American Standard Bible renders it, *"You smear with lies."* The Hebrew lends itself to our idea of whitewashing. Job is accusing the three of "whitewashing" God's actions.

Oh that you would keep silent, (Job 13:5a)

(Remember, in the beginning when you sat with me for seven days and nights.)

> ... it would be your wisdom! Hear now my argument and listen to the pleadings of my lips. Will you speak falsely for God and speak deceitfully for him? Will you show partiality toward him? Will you plead the case for God? Will it be well with you when he searches you out? Or can you deceive him, as one deceives a man? He will surely rebuke you if in secret you show partiality. Will not his majesty terrify you, and the dread of him fall upon you? (Job 13:5b-11)

We know far more of "lying for God" than we care to admit. Some display phony miracles; there are invented healings; religious promoters embellish victories; we indulge in spiritual-sounding boasting. "Neat" answers that attempt to defend God's ways or make Him look good are put forth by His misguided servants. What a small God! Does He need our lies? If we reduce God to this, it should scare us to death!

DEFENDING GOD'S WAYS

Many years ago as the pastor of a small church in Melrose Park, Illinois, I hungered for more visible evidence that God was "at work" in my ministry. Namely, I wanted more response to my invitations and altar calls. A special pastor friend of mine shared the same longing. We attended a pastor's conference held by a church famed for its number of converts and crowds at the altar. We were dismayed to learn of their tactics, such as people being

Friendly Fire

"set-up" to move forward on cue. Some were selected workers, trained to deal with seekers. They had been instructed to not carry Bibles with them. (They were to place them on the front pew before the service began.) My pastor friend objected to this ploy. The leader met his question with, "Why, that's just 'priming the pump'." I wonder whether God needs, and might even be angry with, such manipulative "flesh stuff."

Another, more subtle example is the following: in the late 1960's, Marian and I attended a conference for pastors and church leaders in Minnesota. A missionary whose husband had been murdered at the hands of Indians in South America was one of the speakers. There had been reports that the Indians who had killed him and his co-workers had been contacted and were being reached for Christ. This made the church-at-large feel as though the men had not died in vain.

As I listened to her speak from the book of Habakkuk, I became uncomfortable. She insisted that no viable contact with the tribesmen had occurred up to that time. She discounted defenses of God's ways that many Christians raised in answer to the question, "Why did God let them die?" To me, she sounded bitter. My spiritual immaturity and prejudice against her honesty of speech blinded me to the profound insights she was sharing. Also, I was not even remotely aware of the lessons we are discovering from Job.

Elisabeth Eliot was pointing out that simplistic answers and empty platitudes did not satisfy her, nor are they pleasing to God, and that He, being the sovereign Lord that He is, does not need our puny defenses.

In God's providence—in the school of deep heartache—I also experienced the worthlessness of platitudes and simplistic answers. I learned experientially that I can and must trust Him when I am overwhelmed by loss and grief, because He *is* God.

Zophar, the Zealot

RISKING INNER HONESTY

Habakkuk voiced Job's same questions: "Why, why, why should the evil Chaldeans be used to punish the more righteous Israelites?"

> You who are of purer eyes than to see evil and cannot look at wrong, (Habakkuk 1:13a)

He found no answer. His concluding declaration of trust is beautiful:

> I hear, and my body trembles; my lips quiver at the sound; rottenness enters into my bones; my legs tremble beneath me. Yet I will quietly wait for the day of trouble to come upon people who invade us. Though the fig tree should not blossom, nor fruit be on the vines, the produce of the olive fail and the fields yield no food, the flock be cut off from the fold and there be no herd in the stalls, yet I will rejoice in the LORD; I will take joy in the God of my salvation. GOD, the Lord, is my strength; he makes my feet like the deer's; he makes me tread on my high places. (Habakkuk 3:16-19)

Job, like Habakkuk and Mrs. Eliot, might be faulted for disrespect in his relationship with God but certainly not for a lack of integrity. In his darkest hour David said of God,

> Against you, you only, have I sinned and done what is evil in your sight, so that you may be justified in your words and blameless in your judgment. Behold, I was brought forth in iniquity, and in sin did my mother conceive me. Behold, you delight in truth in the inward being, and you teach me wisdom in the secret heart. (Psalm 51:4-6)

Job has sharply rebuked the three for their cliché-ridden defenses of God. Could it be that in their trite statements they are really just attempting to defend themselves? We need to "tune in" to the earnest protestings of the person in agony, no matter how uncomfortable it is for us. God can and does.

Friendly Fire

Job aggressively continues his course of risking inner honesty:

> Let me have silence, and I will speak, and let come on me what may. Why should I take my flesh in my teeth and put my life in my hand? Though he slay me, I will hope in him; yet I will argue my ways to his face. (Job 13:13-15)

(I know I am taking a risk talking to and about God like this…he may kill me for it, but I will trust Him anyway.)

(The three are so stuck on what Job is saying *that they are deaf to the faith that he is expressing.*)

> This will be my salvation, (Job 13:16a)

(I will be vindicated!)

COLLOQUY ON EVIL THOUGHTS AND IMPULSES

Consider a dilemma. Often in an intensely difficult situation, someone will say to me, "Pastor, I know I shouldn't ask 'why'. I shouldn't question God and His ways. I know I'm a Christian, but my thoughts are so terrible. Words I'd hate to use come into my mind." What can I tell such a person? "Yes, you ought to be ashamed!" I don't think so.

In addressing this, some have mistakenly misused and misapplied Proverbs 24:9, KJV,

> Even the thought of foolishness is sin.

The NASB more accurately translates,

> The devising [or scheming] of folly is sin.

And, the NKJV puts it,

> The devising of foolishness *is* sin.

Consider Jesus's temptations in the wilderness:

Zophar, the Zealot

> Then Jesus was led up by the Spirit into the wilderness to be tempted by the devil. And after fasting forty days and forty nights, he was hungry. And the tempter came and said to him, "If you are the Son of God, command these stones to become loaves of bread." But he answered, "It is written, 'Man shall not live by bread alone, but by every word that comes from the mouth of God.'" Then the devil took him to the holy city and set him on the pinnacle of the temple and said to him, "If you are the Son of God, throw yourself down, for it is written, 'He will command his angels concerning you,' and 'On their hands they will bear you up, lest you strike your foot against a stone.'" Jesus said to him, "Again it is written, 'You shall not put the Lord your God to the test.'" Again, the devil took him to a very high mountain and showed him all the kingdoms of the world and their glory. And he said to him, "All these I will give you, if you will fall down and worship me." Then Jesus said to him, "Be gone, Satan! For it is written, 'You shall worship the Lord your God and him only shall you serve.'" Then the devil left him, and behold, angels came and were ministering to him. (Matthew 4:1-11)

It is apparent that negative, evil thoughts that flash into our mind are not sinful as such.

> For we do not have a high priest who is unable to sympathize with our weaknesses, but one who in every respect has been tempted as we are, yet without sin. (Hebrews 4:15)

Obviously, evil thoughts did enter Jesus' mind, and He did not deny or repress them. Neither did He "own" them; i.e. admit their validity. He answered each false, anti-God idea with the truth, the Scriptures. There are times when we must pray, "Jesus, I can't stop this stream from hell in my head, but I can turn it over to You." We may have to turn these thoughts to Him again and again. The mental war may not end immediately, but I have learned that the enemy of my soul gets tired of getting "beat-up" by Jesus. The temptations do wane.

Friendly Fire

GOD CAN HANDLE OUR HONESTY

We can be sure that God is big enough to "take" our honest anger and questions and to hold us through the trial. As a husband, father, pastor, and man in the world, I often (yes, often) say, "Father, I'm frustrated, hurting, unhappy, and failing." Everywhere I look my life and ministry seem to me like a messed-up basement. Where do I begin to straighten it all out? Satan whispers to my mind, as he did to Jesus, "What's the use?" Awful, angry thoughts come, unbidden. Jesus did not stop the thoughts, nor can I; however, I do not have to "own" them. In such times I can and do, even with tears, turn to Jesus, thanking Him for the grace that gives me His righteousness and thus God's full acceptance and forgiveness. I whisper, "Lord, if not for Your grace, I'm done. I have no plea but my oneness with You, dear Lord...and that is enough!"

Job felt this way. He was able to deal openly with God and his friends with honest feelings, and God accepted him. We know God said to Job's friends:

> My anger burns against you and against your two friends, for you have not spoken of me what is right, as my servant Job has. (Job 42:7b)

Job *was* ultimately vindicated.

In chapter fourteen, Job finishes his answer to Zophar's diatribe with longing. Again, he speaks to God in the presence of the three.

> If a man dies, shall he live again? All the days of my service I would wait, till my renewal should come. You would call, and I would answer you; you would long for the work of your hands. (Job 14:14-15)

(God, you made me, you must love and want me.)

Zophar, the Zealot

For then you would number my steps; you would not keep watch over my sin; my transgression would be sealed up in a bag, and you would cover over my iniquity. (Job 14:16-17)

As I write this my heart overflows. I say, "Amen!" Job had none of the New Testament teaching of God's grace, yet, what a beautiful expression of his confidence in God's free giving and forgiving.

GROUP STUDY GUIDE AND PERSONAL APPLICATION

1. Summarize Zophar's plan of action for Job. How would you describe this man? What was Job's response to Zophar's words?

2. Job does not believe as his friends do that bad people always suffer and fail. He gives us a vivid picture of the wicked in Job 12:6. What does he say?

3. Job insists that bad things *do* happen to good people. Who does he think is responsible for the things that happen to people? With whom does Job wish to argue his case? Have you ever desired to defend yourself before God?

4. What accusation does Job bring against his friends in Job 13:4? Do they deserve it? How does Job wish they would act instead? Have you ever wished that a friend of yours would have attentive ears rather than ignorant words? Consider how you could best help a hurting friend.

5. It is easy for us to attempt to defend God through fake healings, religious boasting, and by engaging in all manner of things that supposedly make God look good. What does this say about our view of God? Restate Elisabeth Eliot's words about the way in which we are to view God.

Friendly Fire

6. Though faced with great trouble, Habakkuk chose to trust God, to rejoice in his circumstances and even to be joyful. Rewrite his words as found in Habakkuk 3:18-19.

7. What did David have to say of God during his confession of sin? (Psalm 51:4,6) What do David's words reveal about himself? About God?

8. Job expresses his faith in God in Job 13:16. What are his words?

9. In spite of all that has happened to Job and regardless of how unfairly Job feels God has treated him, he declares unswervingly his trust in God. Have you come to the place in your life in which you can trust God no matter what happens to you?

10. Purposely scheming to commit a sin is different than having an evil thought just "pop" into your head. During his forty days in the desert, Jesus was tempted to entertain evil thoughts. How did He handle this temptation? What things can you do to resist temptation when negative thoughts bombard your mind?

11. Satan tempts each of us at times with depressing, ungodly thoughts, but he cannot force us to dwell on them. Job dealt openly and honestly with God about the way he was thinking, and God accepted him. However, it was not so with Job's friends. What did God have to say to them?

12. Job was willing to wait out his hard service to God because of his hope. To what was he looking forward? How does Job say that God will handle his sin?

13. Eliphaz comes back for round two of accusations. What were his grievances against Job this time?

14. Job's listeners were hearing his voice but not his heart. How does a person listen "from the heart?" Is there someone in your life who needs you to listen from your heart today?

Don's Reflections

It was Thanksgiving Day and I was in the car running some errands and listening to the "super-station" in Chicago. The moderator was interviewing a U.S. President from bygone years (as he has done in previous years; i.e., Thomas Jefferson). This particular day he was interviewing Theodore Roosevelt, and as the impersonator talked in the voice of Roosevelt, I picked up on a quote that I had recently read in a biography. I went back and found the quote attributed to Roosevelt, a man who knew what it was to face his critics: "It's not the critic who counts. Not the one who points out how the strong man stumbles, or how the doer of deeds might have done it better. The credit belongs to the man who is actually in the arena whose face is marred with sweat and dust and blood. Who strives valiantly. Who errs and comes up short again and again and again. Who knows the great enthusiasms, the great devotions, and spends himself in a worthy cause. Who, if he fails, at least he fails while daring greatly, so that his place shall never be with those cold and timid souls who know neither victory nor defeat."

Oh, that I (we) could keep this perspective next time I (we) am (are) being criticized. In my experience, the majority of critics are Monday morning quarterbacks who have never known the "agony of defeat or the ecstasy of victory." Most have never fought the battle in the arena of faith, making an eternal difference. Dear friend, if your face is beaten and bloodied from life's devastating blows, it is probably because you have been between the lines, in the game, serving God and living for His glory, making a difference.

Friendly Fire

Another one of the cornerstone verses of Job appears in the 13th chapter. It is often quoted, most times misquoted, and more often misunderstood. The King James Version renders the 15th verse as, "Though he slay me, yet I will trust in him." A noble thought and one that exemplifies Job's experience much of the time. Most likely this is not what Job said at this point. The context dictates that Job was getting ready to go into the presence of God. To barge uninvited into the presence of an Oriental King often resulted in death. Job knew that death might be the result of his present course of action. Now, as Pastor Johnson suggests in the text, hit the "pause" button in our drama and "fast forward" to 2 Kings 7:4, and we can liken Job's attitude to that of the four lepers at the Samarian gate who, as they decided to go into the Syrian camp, said, "If they kill us we shall but die." These four lepers, already sentenced to death because of their disease, knew their situation was desperate. Accordingly, they decided to surrender to the Syrians. With death already staring them in the face, what did they have to lose by going over to the enemy camp?

Such was Job's plight. He knew that if he did nothing he would surely die on the ash heap. If he charged into God's presence he could surely die, but there was always that chance that God might be available. Job was determined to pursue his quest. The Revised Standard Version more accurately renders this verse as: "Behold, he will slay me; I have no hope; yet I will defend my ways to his face."

As I have walked through the experiences of life (i.e., death of parents, deaths of close relatives and loved ones, life threatening illnesses and accidents, loss of job, career changes, many critics) I, as well as I am sure you, have frequently wanted to cry out to God with "Why?" "What are you doing, God?" Or, "Where are you, God?" Most times there are no revealed pat answers and so I rest with the prophet Habakkuk when God told him that "... I am do-

Zophar, the Zealot

ing a work in your days that you would not believe if told" (Hab. 1:5).

Therefore, with that understood, I am willing to accept my circumstances even though I am not happy with them. However, God, I would like to plead my case to you sometime in the future and ask that you, in Your grace, give me some answers (my paraphrased understanding of Job 13:15).

Behold, I cry out, "Violence!" but I am not answered; I call for help, but there is no justice.

                              Job 19:7

5

The Battlepoint

The Key: It is easy for one to be self-righteous and believe that if life "seems to be working" for us, it is because we are "doing things right." The truth is, it is grace—all grace.

If it was not for the deep legalistic bias of Job's *comforters*, they surely would have melted, maybe reached out and touched him, apologizing for not "hearing his heart." However, no one is hearing, so the conflict escalates, and Eliphaz hits Job a second time:

> Should a wise man answer with windy knowledge, and fill his belly with the east wind? Should he argue in unprofitable talk, or in words with which he can do no good? (Job 15:2-3)

Friendly Fire

You are just "hot air," Job. (Job scored big when he said in 6:26, [Don't you know that] "the speech of a despairing man is wind?") They cannot let that go without some reply.

Eliphaz continues to hammer,

> But you are doing away with the fear of God and hindering meditation before God. For your iniquity teaches your mouth, and you choose the tongue of the crafty. Your own mouth condemns you, and not I; your own lips testify against you. (Job 15:4-6)

(You are on the side of the wicked.)

> Are the comforts of God too small for you, or the word that deals gently with you? Why does your heart carry you away, and why do your eyes flash, that you turn your spirit against God and bring such words out of your mouth? (Job 15:11-13)

Eliphaz's guilt–pushing goes on without relief to the end of chapter fifteen. They surely do want to shut up Job! I wonder how many of us think it would be better if Job had just buried his feelings? The psychologists would call that "repression." When persistent repression continues, it becomes denial; i.e., we can retreat so far from reality that we begin to believe what is not true. The problem is, when we bury repressed thoughts, they are not *dead* but still alive. They do not go away. They just move "out of focus." Sooner or later reality presses the right buttons and the *buried* thoughts come roaring back, even harder to handle than before.

One of Jesus' Beatitudes is pertinent here. He said,

> Blessed are those who mourn, for they shall be comforted. (Matthew 5:4)

There are six words used in the Greek New Testament that Jesus could have used. He chose the only word that means, "to mourn and *get it out;*" express it, say it with sack cloth and ashes,

The Battlepoint

but *get it out!* Whatever the heartache or disappointment, whether it is your own sins or sins committed against you, get it out.

To hold it in, to pretend it never happened, or that it does not hurt or is not important is "burying it alive." Jesus Christ alive in us can cleanse and empower, but we have to face our thoughts and feelings honestly.

> If we confess our sins [faults, hurts, weaknesses], he is faithful and just to forgive us our sins and to cleanse us from all unrighteousness. (1 John 1:9)

> Therefore, confess your sins to one another and pray for one another, that you may be healed. (James 5:16a)

CONFRONTING TEMPTATION HONESTLY

In the mid 1960's, I became acquainted with the importance of this truth through a friend who held a youth seminar at our church where I had only recently begun my ministry. The group of young people who were "in place" when I came to the church seemed to be "mixed" in their degree of commitment to Christ.

The notes that the leader gave them for the week of lessons comprised an excellent compendium of Scriptural knowledge, yet something troubled me though it was hard to put my finger on what it was. The closing lessons were on victory in the sexual problems and temptations that teenagers experience. The last lesson emphasized the truth that the flesh is responsive to things of the flesh, but the spirit is responsive to things of the Spirit. It sounded good. "So then," he taught, "put away from you tempting things, such as pornography and compromising situations. Pray and memorize Scripture on self-control and purity. The more Scripture you memorize and the more you pray, the closer you will come to God and the less you will have those impulses bothering you."

Friendly Fire

I remember well the pulls and temptations of those teen-age years. As earnest young Christians, my future wife and I met and began dating at the tender age of fifteen. Thankfully, I had to leave home and serve my country during World War II. That separation served us well until we were old enough to marry.

When I heard the lesson being taught these young people, I thought to myself, "I know what is happening here. These kids are buying this and are thinking, 'I'll get closer to God by praying more and memorizing the verses. I'll *do* this. I'll work at it so that I can overcome this temptation to sin. I want to be right with God'." It sounded so good, except I knew that every time they had a sexual impulse, a "red flag" would go up in the back of their mind signaling, "You're a bad guy/girl." If they reach out and hold hands or kiss good-night, more "red flags." (Obviously, these "feelings" are part of the way God made us. How to keep them under His control is the issue here.)

The young person prays, reads and studies more, but the impulses do not go away. Satan whispers, "Look at all those 'red flags!' You are not going to make it through; you are no good. What's the use? You're a bad guy/girl, so go ahead and blow it. There's no hope for you." Then comes a really strong temptation and opportunity to sin. All the "red flags" go up at once. Rather than this being a formula for sexual victory, it is a formula for disaster. Repression is a weak and human response to sin-caused problems. As such it makes us vulnerable to Satan's lies. He loves it when we are *trying hard and doing the best we can.* He knows the truth of Jesus' words,

Apart from me you can do nothing. (John 15:5b)

To *try* to push down or deny what is in the heart (hate, hurt, envy, sinful feelings, thoughts, words and temptations) is powerless. To expect the mere *activities* of praying and Scripture memo-

The Battlepoint

rizing to eliminate them is still without strength. There is no strength in our "doing religion." But what does one do? What is powerful enough?

Certainly God's Word, the Bible, is the Christian's sword and shield. Prayer is our privileged fellowship with our living Lord. **But, He, Himself is our only sufficient strength.**

Paul prayed for the Ephesian Christians and for us:

> I do not cease to give thanks for you, remembering you in my prayers, that the God of our Lord Jesus Christ, the Father of glory, may give you a spirit of wisdom and of revelation in the knowledge of him, having the eyes of your hearts enlightened, that you may know what is the hope to which he has called you, what are the riches of his glorious inheritance in the saints, and what is the immeasurable greatness of his power toward us who believe, according to the working of his great might that he worked in Christ when he raised him from the dead and seated him at his right hand in the heavenly places, (Ephesians 1:16-20)

> [I pray] that according to the riches of his glory he may grant you to be strengthened with power through his Spirit in your inner being, so that Christ may dwell in your hearts through faith—that you, being rooted and grounded in love, may have strength to comprehend with all the saints what is the breadth and length and height and depth, and to know the love of Christ that surpasses knowledge, that you may be filled with all the fullness of God. (Ephesians 3:16-19)

WALKING BY MEANS OF THE SPIRIT

What then does a healthy response to temptation look like? I allow the evil to come into my consciousness, for if I *try* to keep it out, it becomes empowered, multiplying like rats in a dark cellar. I face honestly that yielding to this temptation would be sin. I

Friendly Fire

"mourn and get it out," saying something like, "Jesus, I do not want this to rule my mind. I choose to turn it over to You. I transfer my concentration *from my behaviors* (doing or not doing) to You, expecting (believing, having faith) that You, working in me mightily, have set me free. I thank You for a work done in my being and *walk (live moment by moment) by means of the Spirit* in a fellowship with you—possible only because of Jesus in me through the Holy Spirit." An abundance of Scripture describes this experience:

> But I say, walk by the Spirit, and you will not gratify the desires of the flesh. For the desires of the flesh are against the Spirit, and the desires of the Spirit are against the flesh, for these are opposed to each other, to keep you from doing the things you want to do. But if you are led by the Spirit, you are not under the law. (Galatians 5:16-18)

The Apostle Peter in the first Christian sermon ever preached announces the presence of the risen Christ in every believer:

> For David says concerning him, "I saw the Lord always before me, for he is at my right hand that I may not be shaken;...You have made known to me the paths of life; you will make me full of gladness with your presence." (Acts 2:25,28)

The writer of the Book of Hebrews affirms this truth:

> Keep your life free from love of money, and be content with what you have, for he has said, "I will never leave you nor forsake you." (Hebrews 13:5)

Paul, the Apostle, prays that the Christian will experience the power of this truth:

> [I pray that] having the eyes of your hearts enlightened, that you may know what is the hope to which he has called you, what are the riches of his glorious inheritance in the saints, and what is

The Battlepoint

the immeasurable greatness of his power toward us who believe, according to the working of his great might that he worked in Christ when he raised him from the dead and seated him at his right hand in the heavenly places, far above all rule and authority and power and dominion, and above every name that is named, not only in this age but also in the one to come. (Ephesians 1:18-21)

And finally a promise in a doxology:

Now to him who is able to do far more abundantly than all that we ask or think, according to the power at work within us, to him be glory in the church and in Christ Jesus throughout all generations, forever and ever. Amen. (Ephesians 3:20-21)

We pick up Eliphaz's redundant reasoning,

Listen, Job, let me tell you what I have seen, and other wise men have declared as well; all his days, the wicked man suffers torment. Distress and pain fill him with terror. He may be fat, but his wealth will not endure. He will be like a vine stripped of its unripe grapes. Fire will consume his tents. (Paraphrase of Job 15:17-35)

Longing for an Intercessor

Eliphaz is correct. Certainly evil has its consequences, but often not in this life.

Job answers,

I have heard many such things; miserable comforters are you all. Shall windy words have an end? Or what provokes you that you answer? I also could speak as you do, if you were in my place; I could join words together against you and shake my head at you. I could strengthen you with my mouth, and the solace of my lips would assuage your pain. If I speak, my pain is not assuaged, and if I forbear, how much of it leaves me? (Job 16:2-6)

Friendly Fire

Your theory of God punishing the *bad guys* and blessing the *good guys* is not real to me.

> He has torn me in his wrath and hated me; he has gnashed his teeth at me; my adversary sharpens his eyes against me...I was at ease, and he broke me apart; he seized me by the neck and dashed me to pieces; he set me up as his target; his archers surround me. He slashes open my kidneys and does not spare; he pours out my gall on the ground. He breaks me with breach upon breach; he runs upon me like a warrior. (Job 16:9,12-14)

Job is crying out,

> Even now, behold, my witness is in heaven, and he who testifies for me is on high. My friends scorn me; my eye pours out tears to God, that he would argue the case of a man with God, as a son of man does with his neighbor...My spirit is broken; my days are extinct; the graveyard is ready for me. (Job 16:19-21;17:1)

Again we see how deeply Job longed for an intercessor. In the midst of this pain, his faith moves my heart. We know this intercessor; His name is Jesus, because He lives forever

> Consequently, he is able to save to the uttermost those who draw near to God through him, since he always lives to make intercession for them. (Hebrews 7:25)

My heart wants to sing,

> Jesus, what a friend of sinners,
> Jesus! Lover of my soul;
> Friends may fail me, foes assail me.
> [*Job thought his assailant was God;*
> *We know it was Satan.*]
> He, my Savior, makes me whole.
>
> Hallelujah! What a Savior!
> Hallelujah! What a friend!

Saving me, helping me, keeping me, loving me;
He is with me to the end.[5]

In chapter eighteen, Bildad re-enters the argument by answering Job with the same boring repetition. Although it is sad, it seems so easy for us to be like Bildad—self-righteous with the belief that if life for us is rather comfortable, it is because we are "doing it right." The truth is, it is grace...all grace.

COLLOQUY ON THE BATTLEPOINT

A drama is intriguing because we become involved with the characters. We care what happens to them. Thus, we have empathy for Job. For less cause, we have felt some of the same outrage and anger he is expressing.

In chapter nineteen Job is slipping down an emotional cliff into a pit. Our concern for him is growing heavier.

> How long will you torment me and break me in pieces with words? These ten times you have cast reproach upon me; are you not ashamed to wrong me? (Job 19:2-3)

> Behold, I cry out, "Violence!" but I am not answered; I call for help, but there is no justice. (Job 19:7)

> He has kindled his wrath against me and counts me as his adversary. His troops come on together; they have cast up their siege ramp against me and encamp around my tent. (Job 19:11-12)

Job now recites a catalogue of losses and describes the sense of isolation that comes to one who is terminally ill:

> He has put my brothers far from me, and those who knew me are wholly estranged from me. My relatives have failed me, my close friends have forgotten me. The guests in my house and my maid-

---
[5] J. Wilbur Chapman (1859-1918), *Our Great Savior*.

> servants count me as a stranger; I have become a foreigner in their eyes. I call to my servant, but he gives me no answer; I must plead with him with my mouth for mercy. My breath is strange to my wife, and I am a stench to the children of my own mother. Even young children despise me; when I rise they talk against me. All my intimate friends abhor me, and those whom I loved have turned against me. My bones stick to my skin and to my flesh, and I have escaped by the skin of my teeth. (Job 19:13-20)

Job hits the bottom.

> Have mercy on me, have mercy on me, O you my friends, for the hand of God has touched me! Why do you, like God, pursue me? (Job 19:21-22a)

Why has God made me His enemy, His "target?" For Job the days of suffering are piling up. The pain, fear, worry, despair, and fighting have caught up with him. He is exhausted, and he begs for pity.

Job's Great Faith and Testimony

There is a break between vv. 22 and 23, though it is not as evident in the text itself as much as it is in the sense of the drama. Job is exhausted, momentarily overcome with emotion. I can imagine his turning away from his friends. Then, before they can answer, he flies from the depth of the pit to the mountain top. If we were actually watching this drama being enacted on a stage, background music would indicate a mounting tension. A climax is coming.

> Oh that my words were written! Oh that they were inscribed in a book! Oh that with an iron pen and lead they were engraved in the rock forever! (Job 19:23-24)

Write them down **now,** because I do not always feel this way. **Now,** with my convictions and feelings together, put what I say

The Battlepoint

into a book. **No**! A book or scroll is too perishable. I may not feel like this later, but *this* is what I am. *This* is my hope.

Then Job pours out words that call to mind Handel's *Messiah*.

> For I know that my Redeemer lives, and at the last he will stand upon the earth. (Job 19:25)

> And I will stand with Him!!

> And after my skin has been thus destroyed, yet in my flesh I shall see God, whom I shall see for myself, and my eyes shall behold, and not another. My heart faints within me! (Job 19:26-27)

By now we are cheering for Job. Where is there a more magnificent example of genuine faith? Job's perseverance is a tremendous encouragement to us. He says, "If it takes eternity to prove it, so be it! If I don't understand until I stand with Him, I will then."

This is a faith that reaches out beyond present pain and puzzlement and, while facing inner turmoil honestly, can still receive victory. In times of trial and temptation, we do not have to pretend that we are not hurting, nor do we have to be ashamed. We turn to Jesus. There is comfort *now* and the promise that if it takes eternity to realize it, God's love has not failed.

> Who shall separate us from the love of Christ? Shall tribulation, or distress, or persecution, or famine, or nakedness, or danger, or sword? As it is written, "For your sake we are being killed all the day long; we are regarded as sheep to be slaughtered." No, in all these things we are more than conquerors through him who loved us. For I am sure that neither death nor life, nor angels nor rulers, nor things present nor things to come, nor powers, nor height nor depth, nor anything else in all creation, will be able to separate us from the love of God in Christ Jesus our Lord. (Romans 8:35-39)

Friendly Fire

GROUP STUDY GUIDE AND PERSONAL APPLICATION

1. In the Beatitudes Jesus said, "Blessed are those who mourn, for they will be comforted." Explain what Jesus meant by choosing this particular meaning of the word "mourn." Describe what is likely to happen to a person who suffers but does not mourn.

2. How important it is that we honestly recognize our needs and present them to God for His help. What do 1 John 1:19 and James 5:16 teach us about God's response to our honest confession? Do you find these verses personally comforting to you?

3. In an earnest desire to be good, to try hard, and to resist temptation, we may actually be setting ourselves up for failure. What vital thing do we need to remember?

4. Prayer and Bible reading are essential to a believer's life, but only Jesus Himself can empower us to live godly lives. When Paul prayed for the Ephesian church, what did he ask God to give to the people?

5. When Christ becomes the dominating factor in our behavior and He begins to empower us, what will we be able to do according to Ephesians 3:16-19?

6. Rehearse briefly the steps a believer can take when faced with temptation.

7. Discuss what Paul meant when he exhorted believers in Galatians 5:16 to "live by the Spirit." Share with the group the conflict you experience between your sinful nature and the new nature you received when you gave your life to Christ.

8. Every believer has Christ indwelling him and directing him. What precious promise does He give us in Hebrews 13:5? How can this verse help you when you face trials in your life?

The Battlepoint

9. With Christ's power at work in us, what does Ephesians 3:20 tell us He is able to do in our lives? Can you recall a situation in your life in which God enabled you to do something you never dreamed you would be able to do?

10. Job longed for our intercessor Jesus. What does Hebrews 7:24-25 tell us that Jesus does for believers?

11. Physical and emotional suffering bring Job to a new low. Exhausted, he wishes for his words to be recorded forever. Then in a great outpouring of his soul, Job proclaims the words written in Job 19:25-27. Write in your own words what Job wants future generations to hear. What was the greatest longing of Job's heart?

12. In the midst of deep pain, we can turn to Jesus, who promises to comfort us and whose love will never fail. List all of the things Romans 8:35-39 tells us will never be able to separate us from Christ's love. Have you received Christ's unfailing love into your life?

Don's Reflections

Donald Grey Barnhouse, a famous pastor from Philadelphia and a prolific writer and author, was quoted as saying, "It is a sad fact that the tongues of professing Christians are often all too busy doing the devil's work."

The unfolding drama of Job's life now comes to the second round of dialogues with his three friends. Instead of listening, comforting, and counseling, his friends were busy regurgitating the same arguments for their retribution theology. They couldn't wait for Job to stop his talking so that they could begin anew with their scathing attack. The dialogue becomes more intense, more impatient and more critical.

Abraham Lincoln once said, "He has the right to criticize who has the heart to help." In other words, it is not enough just to

Friendly Fire

point out another person's shortcomings. Instead, one must be committed to help that person work through his/her problems or failures in order to help him. It has been said that "it takes no size to criticize." Anyone can point out the faults of others. The mark of a truly great person is helping people overcome their shortfalls.

Unfortunately, Job's friends had not come to that place in their lives. They did not have the hearts to help Job. Therefore, they forfeited the right to criticize. An old adage is, "People do not care how much you know until they know how much you care." Job's friends were like noisy gongs and clanging cymbals (1 Cor. 13:1).

Chapter 19 of Job is one of the greatest chapters of the Bible, because it expresses Job's certainty that he eventually will be vindicated, even if this vindication comes after he dies.

Out of the depth of great sorrow and loneliness, Job began to rise to his greatest heights of belief and anticipation. He begins by expressing the wish that his words might be written down in a book; perhaps inscribed on a copper scroll. But what "words" did Job want inscribed in a book or on a rock? Was it his confession in v. 25, "I know that my Redeemer lives"? Or, was it his words about his innocence? I would lean toward the latter. Job wanted his name cleared and his honor vindicated. He had given up hope of such being done during his lifetime. Therefore, he thought of some way of preserving his case so that it could be decided by posterity. He wanted a permanent record to be made of it either on a metal scroll or on a rock. He did not want his case to be buried in a book or hidden in some obscure inscription. He wanted a personal advocate—someone who would go to bat for him, clear his name, and reconcile him with God.

Then in a flash of light as brilliant as the desert sun, Job exclaimed, "But I know that my Redeemer lives!" Every word in that sentence in the Hebrew is emphatic. The "but" is more than a conjunctive. It introduces v. 25 as something different from what has gone before. Pastor Johnson would often teach that everything before the "but" is canceled out and what follows the "but" now stands in its place. In effect, Job said, "I could wish for my case to be written in a book or on a rock, <u>but</u> there is something better than that; namely, a living Redeemer." Additionally, the "I" is emphatic in the Hebrew and the word "know" is to "know by experience."

The word "redeemer" in v. 25 is the Hebrew word, *go'el*. It is used of a man, the next of kin, who acts as the avenger of blood in the case of a murder. It is used for the redeemer of a kinsman who has been sold into slavery. In some cases the *go'el* redeemed the property of this kinsman and married his widow to raise up children to bear his name. Sometimes God is called Israel's *Go'el*.

The question arises as to whether Job was speaking of a human *go'el* or of a divine *Go'el*. It seems to me that Job had given up all hope in man's ability and willingness to justify him. He turned toward heaven, but God was his enemy (he thought). He believed that God was responsible for all of his trouble (which is true in a sense). Therefore, Job returned to his earlier thoughts of an umpire (9:23) and a heavenly witness (16:19). He advanced to the concept of a living Redeemer (19:25), a "vindication." The kind of redeemer Job envisioned would have to be one who would not die, as he was about to do, but one who would at last "stand upon the earth." Even after Job died, such a Redeemer would usher him into the presence of God, where from his flesh he would see God (19:26). This is what is known as "finishing well."

William Booth, the founder of the Salvation Army in London, persevered faithfully to the end of his life. At age 82 and almost blind, Booth stood before an audience of 10,000 at Royal Albert Hall in London and gave his last public address. His final words

Friendly Fire

reveal an unbreakable faith that remained steadfast to the Lord, firm to the finish.

> While women weep as they do, I will fight.
> While children go hungry as they do, I will fight.
> While there is a drunkard left, I will fight.
> While there is a poor girl left on the streets, I will fight.
> While there remains one dark soul without the light of God, I will fight.
> I will fight—I will fight to the very end.

True faith presses on to the end. Such was William Booth's faith. Such was Job's faith, and such must be our faith as well.

My wife Sharon has been involved in a ministry to one of the young mothers in our congregation who has been diagnosed with a severe case of cancer. For the last seven years Kim has had hundreds of treatments. Remissions and reoccurrences have been numerous. Just when you might think she is about to step into the presence of Jesus and have all pain removed, she rallies and continues the fight. Her faith, and that of Bill, her husband, has been tried and tested time after time. Through it all she proclaims how good God is! As I write this, she is in the hospital—admitted because of seizures caused by the ravaging disease.

With four young daughters and a husband who has been through the mill, our hearts continually go out to them. Numerous persons in the congregation have volunteered help. Sharon, along with ministering to her spiritual needs also assists in driving Kim to chemotherapy and MRI appointments. Certainly, here is a family that can stand with Job and ask, "Why is God shooting at us?" We know, and Kim knows, that God is the Great Physician. Human doctors have no explanation as to what keeps her going. We have a saying at Moraine, "It is a NEEG experience (No Explanation Except God)!" We know, and Kim knows, that God is

The Battlepoint

the Conqueror of death. What we don't know is how many souls have been saved, restored, strengthened and touched by the faith of this great soldier. True faith presses on to the end!

Because God has loosed my cord and humbled me, they have cast off restraint in my presence. On my right hand the rabble rise; they push away my feet; they cast up against me their ways of destruction.

Job 30:11-12

6

God, Why Are You Shooting at Me?

Or,"Why God Permits Bad Things to Happen to His People."

> *The Key: God can and will entrust to us the assignment of being a battlepoint. He will bring glory to Himself in the victories we experience through His working.*

Friendly Fire is a dreadful term. I heard it first when it described an infantry attack in the Solomon Islands during World War II. When a company landed on the beach, they expected air support to strafe and bomb the enemy in front of them, so they dug in and waited. American planes appeared on the horizon. Fire spit from the wing guns of the attacking fighter planes. The pilots had received erroneous instructions or else they had mis-

Friendly Fire

identified the target. Fire power hit their own soldiers instead of the enemy. Small anti-personnel bombs burst on the beach. The rising cheers of the infantrymen evaporated as they realized that they had become the target. Those waiting in their foxholes were blown out. Those not hit ran in confusion. A reporter wrote, "It looked as if someone had messed up an ant hill." It was tragic.

More recently in the Mideast two helicopters carrying high-ranking officers were shot down by two American fighter pilots who misidentified the copters as being of Russian manufacture. Twenty-six people were lost to "friendly fire." There were investigations to ascertain the blame; mistakes were admitted. The official explanations were that this was human error, a terrible side effect of war.

We feel the tragedy. To be brutally attacked by your own side seems inexcusable. It must be a mistake.

This is the way Job felt toward God. "Why are you making me a target? Why are you shooting at me?"

> For the arrows of the Almighty are in me; my spirit drinks their poison; (Job 6:4a)

> If I sin, what do I do to you, you watcher of mankind? Why have you made me your mark? Why have I become a burden to you? (Job 7:20)

> Why do you hide your face and count me as your enemy? (Job 13:24)

> He has torn me in his wrath and hated me; he has gnashed his teeth at me; my adversary sharpens his eyes against me...his archers surround me. He slashes open my kidneys and does not spare; he pours out my gall on the ground. (Job 16:9,13)

> He has kindled his wrath against me and counts me as his adversary. His troops come on together; they have cast up their

siege ramp against me and encamp around my tent. (Job 19:11-12)

Because God has loosed my cord and humbled me, they have cast off restraint in my presence. On my right hand the rabble rise; they push away my feet; they cast up against me their ways of destruction. (Job 30:11-12)

Behold, he finds occasions against me, he counts me as his enemy, (Job 33:10)

The explanation that evil is a part of life may hold up for the times when life is smooth, but it is an inadequate answer to Job's question, "Why do bad things happen to good people like me?"

We attempt to answer this difficult question in several ways.

TESTING

God is testing *us*. Tests and trials are not for God's sake, but for ours. He knows the way in which we will hold up, but without being tested, *we* do not.

> More than that, we rejoice in our sufferings, knowing that suffering produces endurance, and endurance produces character, and character produces hope, (Romans 5:3-4)

> [For] you know that the testing of your faith produces steadfastness. And let steadfastness have its full effect, that you may be perfect and complete, lacking in nothing. (James 1:3-4)

Job reaches out beyond his feelings to his beliefs. He says,

> But he knows the way that I take; when he has tried me, I shall come out as gold...I have not departed from the commandment of his lips; I have treasured the words of his mouth more than my portion of food. (Job 23:10,12)

Sincere Christians can expect to be tested so that *we* may be confident of His strength in us for anything!

BROKENNESS

The opposite of brokenness is self-sufficiency. Therefore, as a good and wise Father, God will work toward "brokenness" in the lives of every one of His loved children. His Word says,

> It is for discipline that you have to endure. God is treating you as sons. For what son is there whom his father does not discipline? If you are left without discipline [and everyone undergoes discipline], in which all have participated, then you are illegitimate children and not sons. Besides this, we have had earthly fathers who disciplined us and we respected them. Shall we not much more be subject to the Father of spirits and live? For they disciplined us for a short time as it seemed best to them, but he disciplines us for our good, that we may share his holiness. For the moment all discipline seems painful rather than pleasant, but later it yields the peaceful fruit of righteousness to those who have been trained by it. (Hebrews 12:7-11)

So, God is testing and refining us; He is lovingly disciplining us to a broken dependence on Him. However, there is more. Needing and receiving grace *breaks* us. The more clearly we perceive the weakness of our humanity and its imagined strengths, the more attractive and necessary brokenness becomes. The believing heart realizes brokenness through the Father's training, then Grace flows into and out of our lives.

SPIRITUAL CONFLICT

My favorite recreational reading has been in the area of military science and tactics. I like battle stories, heroism, strategy development and biography. Douglas MacArthur and Omar Bradley were great leaders and their stories are an inspiration. I recall reading of the research and anguish Bradley and his aides experienced in selecting the battlepoints for the "D-Day" invasion of

God, Why Are You Shooting at Me?

Europe. Strategy dictates that a good general choose the battlepoint, for he would not want to fight on the enemy's terms.

God can and does choose one of His loved children to become a "battlepoint" at strategic times. Our painful experiences at these times might seem like "friendly fire." So it was with Job; he felt like a *target*. This is the deepest answer to the problem of the reason God chooses to put His loved child through heartache, pain and loss.

Most of our world and many Christians are poorly informed regarding spiritual warfare, as were Job and his friends. There is little recognition that the tragic condition of life on earth and human behavior in general is the result of this spiritual conflict. This war has been waged in the realm of the spirit from the beginning. I am not referring to the occult and specific demonic workings, for daily we all deal with Satan's attack in our minds. Jesus' battle with Satan in the wilderness is a prototype of the battle we continually fight. The Christian life cannot be fully understood without addressing this warfare.

We must be aware of the scriptural instruction regarding conflict. The New Testament witness to this inner personal warfare is massive. One notable mention is the place in which Jesus warns Peter that Satan desires to subvert Him, just as he plotted to destroy Job thousands of years earlier.

> Simon, Simon, behold, Satan demanded to have you, that he might sift you like wheat, but I have prayed for you that your faith may not fail. (Luke 22:31-32a)

The Apostle Paul writes,

> In their case the god of this world has blinded the minds of the unbelievers, to keep them from seeing the light of the gospel of the glory of Christ, who is the image of God. (2 Corinthians 4:4)

In Ephesians he warns,

Friendly Fire

> Finally, be strong in the Lord and in the strength of his might. Put on the whole armor of God, that you may be able to stand against the schemes of the devil. For we do not wrestle against flesh and blood, but against the rulers, against the authorities, against the cosmic powers over this present darkness, against the spiritual forces of evil in the heavenly places. (Ephesians 6:10-12)

Because Satan's only hope is to shake the Christian's faith, he challenges Timothy to "fight the good fight of the faith" and "Share in suffering as a good soldier of Christ Jesus." (1 Timothy 1:18; 6:12 and 2 Timothy 2:3-4.)

In his letter, the Apostle James encourages us to

> Submit yourselves therefore to God. Resist the devil, and he will flee from you. (James 4:7)

The Apostle Peter writes,

> Your adversary the devil prowls around like a roaring lion, seeking someone to devour. Resist him, firm in your faith, (1 Peter 5:8b-9a)

The Apostle John affirms that our fight is the fight of *faith* and that overcoming is a result of *faith*.

> Little children, you are from God and have overcome them, for he who is in you is greater than he who is in the world...For everyone who has been born of God overcomes the world. And this is the victory that has overcome the world— our faith. (1 John 4:4; 5:4)

Furthermore, John tells us of Satan's destiny; i.e., hell forever (Rev. 20:10). He teaches that the devil has been sinning from the beginning, and the reason the Son of God came into the world was to destroy the devil's work (1 John 1:8).

There is just no way that any Biblically knowledgeable person can say, "I'll just keep trusting Jesus and not concern myself with the devil." (Be sure that he concerns himself with you.)

God, Why Are You Shooting at Me?

GOD'S TARGET

It seemed to Job that he was a *target* and God was shooting at him. But he did not know of the challenge in heaven that God, in His sovereign love, power and wisdom, had chosen *him* to be a *battlepoint*—a point in time and space on earth and in a human being in which Satan will be permitted to strike. However, Satan will not win; he will be defeated! These defeats of the enemy are beyond counting in number, and each of them brings glory to God.

Satan's onslaughts against Job were his attempts to prove that God cannot satisfy the human soul if material and physical benefits are removed. Mankind first saw this tactic employed in Eden.

It is important and necessary that we understand this tactic today. In that garden Satan, in the serpent, came to Eve and said, "Did God *actually* say, 'You shall not eat of *any* tree in the garden'?" (Genesis 3:1) Note that he plants a doubt.

"Did God *actually* say?" Then he misquotes God's Word. "Did God say don't eat from *any* tree?".

What God did say was, "You are *free* to eat from *any* tree in the garden" except one (Gen. 2:16 NIV)—the opposite of what Satan implied.

Eve helped Satan beguile her by misquoting God:

> And the woman said to the serpent, "We may eat of the fruit of the trees in the garden, but God said, 'You shall not eat of the fruit of the tree that is in the midst of the garden, neither shall you touch it, lest you die.'" (Genesis 3:2-3)

God did not prohibit *touching* the tree. Typical of religious legalists, Eve added what God did not say and thereby weakened what God *did* say. It opened the door for Satan's lie:

> You will not surely die. (Genesis 3:4b)

Friendly Fire

God had lovingly supplied Adam and Eve with everything they needed, including fellowship with Himself. After casting doubt on and then contradicting God's Word, Satan's words to Eve were to persuade her that God and His care were not enough to satisfy and that He was holding out on her.

> For God knows that when you eat of it your eyes will be opened, and you will be like God, knowing good and evil. (Genesis 3:5)

This was the very strategy used against Jesus when Satan tempted Him in the wilderness (Matthew 4:1-11), and he uses it continually against believers today. He relentlessly employed it against Job.

> Not withstanding Satan's power and strategy, the book of Job teaches us that by bringing Job, and many of us like him, through suffering and loss triumphantly, God is saying, 'In a world where prosperity, luxury and comfort are the aim of most effort...health and happiness, the object of most prayer...companionship of family and friends, the highest fellowship...I will permit the enemy to touch you and take them from you, yet you will overcome! I will stand with you, My promises will hold you. Not only will you win, but for thousands of years to come, and in many believers' lives, your triumph will bring honor to me; and Satan will have a mouthful of dust for his efforts.[6]

THE BATTLEPOINT

Now we have a new answer to the question, "Why do bad things happen to God's people?" God can and will entrust to us the as-

---

[6] This magnificent quote is from what I gleaned from my notes of Dr. William Hulme's lectures.

God, Why Are You Shooting at Me?

signment of being a battlepoint. He will bring glory to Himself in the victories we experience through His mighty working in us.

It strengthens us to remember that God has chosen some of His choice children to be battlepoints.

Joseph was a patriarch of Israel and a favored son of his father Jacob. Like Job, he had a reputation for godly character. His only possible flaw might have been misjudging his brothers' reaction when he told them his dream about the whole family's bowing down to him.

One day Jacob sent Joseph out to the fields to check on his brothers' welfare and work habits. The brothers, angry because of Joseph's apparent conceit and envious because of their father's favoritism, plotted to kill him. Reuben, Jacob's first son and the one who should have been treated as the favorite, intervened, declaring that *no blood should be shed*. Intending to return later and rescue Joseph, he suggested that his brother be thrown into a dried-up well and left to die. Some time later, while Reuben was away, the brothers pulled Joseph out of the well and sold him as a slave to a caravan headed for Egypt. I can imagine that Joseph, about seventeen at the time, bouncing on camel-back and in chains, was frightened, and filled with pain, abandonment and despair. In Egypt, one of Pharaoh's officers bought Joseph, who did so well that Potiphar turned the management of his estate over to him.

However, Potiphar's wife was attracted to Joseph and tried to seduce him. He refused her and fled in protest:

> How then can I do this great wickedness and sin against God? (Genesis 39:9b)

As Joseph fled, the woman grabbed part of his clothing which he slipped out of and left behind. Angry and rejected, she shrieked for help. Waving Joseph's garment to prove he had

Friendly Fire

forced himself on her, she had him thrown into prison. As he sat there with his head in his hands, he surely felt like Job. He would question, as did Job, "What does it benefit me to be a godly person?"

> What is the Almighty, that we should serve him? And what profit do we get if we pray to him? (Job 21:15)

> For he has said, "It profits a man nothing that he should take delight in God." (Job 34:9)

> ...you ask, "What advantage have I? How am I better off than if I had sinned?" (Job 35:3)

While in that prison, Joseph received a God-given ability to interpret dreams. After two full years, Pharaoh had a dream and remembered Joseph, who accurately interpreted his dream and became Pharaoh's prime minister.

Joseph's interpretation of the dream enabled Egypt to prepare for a seven-year famine which spread to the whole known earth. In the land of Canaan, Joseph's brothers were compelled to seek the purchase of food from Egypt. They journeyed there and were granted an audience with the prime minister, for Pharaoh had decreed,

> ...I am Pharaoh, and without your consent no one shall lift up hand or foot in all the land of Egypt. (Genesis 41:44)

Joseph recognized his brothers and capitalized on the fact that they did not recognize him. Joseph devised a series of tests to slowly reveal himself to his brothers. Once they recognized him, they reasoned that while their father Jacob lived, they were safe from Joseph's retaliation. However, when Jacob died, fear struck the brothers' hearts. Now they had reason to worry that Joseph would pay them back in full for all the wrong they had done to him.

God, Why Are You Shooting at Me?

> When Joseph's brothers saw that their father was dead, they said, "It may be that Joseph will hate us and pay us back for all the evil that we did to him." (Genesis 50:15)

They sent a message admitting their sin and asking forgiveness. Upon receiving the message, Joseph wept.

> His brothers also came and fell down before him and said, "Behold, we are your servants." (Genesis 50:18)

Joseph's response to them is a powerful and touching example of the *battlepoint*.

> But Joseph said to them, "Do not fear, for am I in the place of God? As for you, you meant evil against me, but God meant it for good, to bring it about that many people should be kept alive, as they are today. So do not fear; I will provide for you and your little ones." Thus he comforted them and spoke kindly to them. (Genesis 50:19-21)

Through the triumph of Joseph's faith in adversity, God saved many lives and brought glory to Himself.

JESUS: THE ULTIMATE BATTLEPOINT

Four hundred thirty years later, the descendants of Joseph, now slaves in Egypt, are about to be delivered from their crushing situation. God uses Moses and Aaron to confront the Pharaoh of that time. Because the slave labor was profitable, Pharaoh refused again and again to let them go. Finally, God sent the angel of death to take the lives of the firstborn in each home not protected by the blood sprinkled on the door of the home.

When Pharaoh finally relented and gave them permission to leave, they prepared and moved out. Pharaoh then changed his mind and pursued them with his mighty army. The fleeing Israelites came to the Red Sea, but there was no way of escape. Then, the battle-point:

Friendly Fire

> Then the LORD said to Moses, "Tell the people of Israel to turn back and encamp in front of Pi-hahiroth, between Migdol and the sea, in front of Baal-zephon; you shall encamp facing it, by the sea. For Pharaoh will say of the people of Israel, 'They are wandering in the land; the wilderness has shut them in.' And I will harden Pharaoh's heart, and he will pursue them, and I will get glory over Pharaoh and all his host, and the Egyptians shall know that I am the LORD." And they did so. (Exodus 14:1-4)

Satan is defeated and God is glorified through the faith of God's chosen battlepoint.

It is encouraging to realize that this is what the Apostle Paul experienced from his jail cell. As he faced execution, he wrote to the Philippian Church:

> ...it is my eager expectation and hope that I will not be at all ashamed, but that with full courage now as always Christ will be honored in my body, whether by life or by death. (Philippians 1:20)

Even more, we realize Jesus was made the *ultimate* battlepoint as God the Father opened the hedge and let Satan attack Him! He experienced Gethsemane...the cross...the grave...and then...His glorious resurrection. *His* resurrection promises *our* resurrection—*our* ultimate triumph.

I am reminded of a conversation with a Christian brother who had every earthly reason to be cynical. His body had been severely disabled by an automobile accident, and his promising career was decimated. We talked together about what comfort there might be in suffering for "God's glory." (God winning over Satan.) He asked me, "Bill, is God's bringing glory to Himself so important that my life has to be so messed up?" Cannot everyone of us feel this?

Job experienced a glimpse of eternity when he cried, "Engrave it on a rock, **forever!** My Redeemer, My Deliverer lives, and

I will live and stand with Him." The most and the best of human life is not experienced here and now, but in God's *Forever*.

These are not just comforting words for a funeral, but we need to consider that eternity's triumph includes the believer's reward. If you are one who thinks, "I am so glad I am saved from hell; I don't need to know much about rewards," you are missing a great, strengthening encouragement.

Living for and serving Christ yields wonderful rewards along the way. Sometimes it is an insight from Scripture, a special promise at a perfect time, the supply of need that only God could affect, and times of corporate and personal worship during which the sense of His presence and love is almost overwhelming. The heart fills up, and sometimes it leaks out the eyes and the nose. This is part of the "joy of the Lord" that is our strength. (Nehemiah 8:10)

But there is so much more—the reality of future reward. He is saying, "I have the authority to make and keep this promise."

> Behold, I am coming soon, bringing my recompense with me, to repay everyone for what he has done. I am the Alpha and the Omega, the first and the last, the beginning and the end. (Revelation 22:12-13)

GROUP STUDY GUIDE AND PERSONAL APPLICATION

1. Job feels that he has become God's target and that God is angry and finding fault with him unjustly. He wonders why bad things happen to good people. Read Romans 5:3 and James 1:3-4. What are the results of testing and trials? How does Job express hope for his future (Job 23:10)?

Friendly Fire

2. Share with the group a time when you learned a lesson in perseverance as a result of a trial you experienced. Were you able to say that the end result was good?

3. How does Hebrews 12:7-11 teach us we are able to endure hardship? If God never disciplines a person, what can we conclude? What does God's discipline produce in the receptive believer?

4. Define what is meant by *brokenness* in the life of a believer. Why is it necessary?

5. As Christians we must be aware of the spiritual warfare which rages all around us. Satan attempts to subvert and blind people's minds. What specific things can we do to fight in the battle against Satan and win?

6. Using a dictionary, define the word "resist." How does a believer resist the devil? What is Satan's ultimate destiny?

7. Describe Satan's tactics in the garden of Eden. How did Eve further Satan's misleading?

8. God gave Adam and Eve everything they could possibly need, yet Satan deluded them into thinking it was not enough. What did Satan promise Adam and Eve? Summarize Satan's attempts at using that same strategy with Jesus in Matthew 4:1-11. Jesus overcame Satan! What encouragement does that bring you today?

9. Like Job, Joseph got into trouble while leading a godly life. Summarize the question Joseph asked about God.

10. What did Joseph proclaim as the ultimate reason for God's allowing the pain in his life?

11. Good triumphing through adversity is the theme of another Old Testament story in which Moses, Aaron and Pharaoh are the

characters. Briefly describe what happened and how good triumphed.

12. What was Paul's hope during the pain of his prison sentence and impending execution?

13. How did Jesus become the ultimate battlepoint between God the Father and Satan? What hope does Jesus' triumph bring to the lives of His children?

14. Christians are rewarded for standing firm in their faith, both now and in eternity. Share ways in which the Lord has rewarded you for your faithfulness to Him. Have you experienced Nehemiah 8:10?

Don's Reflections

"Why do bad things happen to good people?" This is a question that has been discussed, pondered, books written to try to answer it, but with no certainty! Answers offered comfort the hearts of those not experiencing the "bad things." But for those going through excruciating trials there is little comfort in the words, "He will bring glory to Himself in victories we experience through His mighty working in us." Or, "It strengthens us to remember that God has chosen some of His choice children to be battlepoints" (*Friendly Fire*, p. 111).

I don't mean to belittle these words of comfort, but I sometimes wonder if we don't generally focus on surviving our trials and the attendant blessings that may follow.

It was January 2007. In previous years we would have been visiting our daughter and her family in Arizona by this time. We were late in heading to the Southwest, and I don't remember the reasons why and they matter not. I remember getting a call from my sister, who was visiting one of her children and family in Florida for the holidays. Her voice broke and she sobbed as she

Friendly Fire

said, "Don, Danette was just killed in an automobile accident in Michigan." Danette was one of my sister's married daughters. She and her husband, who had been and still is on disability due to a debilitating disease, have three young children. Danette was on her way to work early in the morning and the roads were slippery. She hit a patch of ice and skidded head-on into the oncoming traffic. She died at the scene of the accident.

Sharon and I and two of our adult children traveled to Michigan for the services. At the funeral home, all I could do was to embrace my sister as she sobbed. I said nothing. My sister cried out, "Don, parents are not supposed to outlive their children—this isn't right!"

My sister and all of her children are believers. Have we seen evidences of God's glory? Certainly! Hundreds and hundreds of people attended the funeral. Witness after witness testified to the strong Christian life lived by Danette and the impact she had in her community and church. I don't think her family had any idea how far her life reached out and how many lives she touched. I am reminded of the story recorded in Matthew 26:6-13 where Jesus says of Mary, who anointed him with expensive perfume, "Truly, I say to you, wherever this gospel is proclaimed in the whole world, what she has done will also be told in memory of her" (v. 13).

We still have questions. The family still hurts. Tears still well up in eyes during conversations about her. But we know that God in His sovereign love, power and wisdom chose Danette and our family to be a "battlepoint"—a point in time and space on earth, and in our human experience, in which Satan was permitted to strike. However, Satan will not win, he will be defeated and in his defeat God will bring glory to Himself.

God, Why Are You Shooting at Me?

I can't say that I understand—I wish I did. But, I believe! I believe that Danette is standing with Job, on shore, as the song says that was sung at her funeral:

> When alarmed by the fury of the restless sea,
> Towering waves before you roll,
> At the end of doubt and peril is eternity,
> Though fear and conflict siege your soul.
>
> Just think of stepping on shore, and finding it heaven
> Of touching a hand, and finding it God's
> Of breathing new air, and finding it celestial
> Of waking up in Glory, and finding it "Home."
>
> When surrounded by the blackness of the darkest night,
> Oh how lonely death can be,
> At the end of this long tunnel is a shining light,
> For death is swallowed-up in victory. (Victory!)
>
> Just think of stepping on shore, and finding it heaven
> Of touching a hand, and finding it God's
> Of breathing new air, and finding it celestial
> Of waking up in Glory, and finding it "Home!"[7]

What confidence we can have! "He knows the way that I take; when he has tried me, I shall come out as gold" (Job 23:10).

---

[7] Don Wyrtzen, *Finally Home.*

But he knows the way that I take; when he has tried me, I shall come out as gold.

>Job 23:10

7

Resurrection Glory and the Believer's Reward

The Key: For the one who trusts Christ now, the best is yet to come.

Job had expressed hope in the resurrection. In the midst of all of his disappointment, pain and confusion he held firmly to the reality of standing before God on the resurrection day.

> For I know *that* my Redeemer lives, And He shall stand at last on the earth; And after my skin is destroyed, this *I know,* that in my flesh I shall see God, whom I shall see for myself, and my eyes shall behold, and not another. *How* my heart yearns within me! (Job 19:25-27 NKJV)

The promise of the angels when Jesus ascended to His Father was that He would return with a physical body as well.

Friendly Fire

> Men of Galilee, why do you stand looking into heaven? This Jesus, who was taken up from you into heaven, will come in the same way as you saw him go into heaven. (Acts 1:11)

A New Body like Jesus' Resurrection Body

We share in the hope of the resurrection and the promise that kept Job's heart: we, too, will stand before the Lord God. Our bodies will one day be like Jesus' own glorious body!

> But our citizenship is in heaven, and from it we await a Savior, the Lord Jesus Christ, who will transform our lowly body to be like his glorious body, by the power that enables him even to subject all things to himself. (Philippians 3:20-21)

The apostle John also set this hope before the people of God. When we see Him, we shall be like Him!

> Beloved, we are God's children now, and what we will be has not yet appeared; but we know that when he appears we shall be like him, because we shall see him as he is. (1 John 3:2)

Jesus' resurrection body is not metaphysical or mystical; rather it is substantial and real. His resurrection life is a conscious continuation of His earthly life. An eternal life without this continuity has little attraction for us. We will have a body as He had when He rose from the dead and ate fish and biscuits with his friends on the shore of the Sea of Galilee. He walked on the earth for six weeks until He was taken, bodily, into heaven from the presence of more than five hundred witnesses.

A Liberated Creation

As well as a substantial resurrection body, the believer's future promises a new physical creation. We can feel the excitement in the Apostle Paul's heart as he writes,

Resurrection Glory and the Believer's Reward

> For I consider that the sufferings of this present time are not worth comparing with the glory that is to be revealed to us. For the creation waits with eager longing for the revealing of the sons of God. For the creation was subjected to futility, not willingly, but because of him who subjected it, in hope that the creation itself will be set free from its bondage to corruption and obtain the freedom of the glory of the children of God. For we know that the whole creation has been groaning together in the pains of childbirth until now. And not only the creation, but we ourselves, who have the firstfruits of the Spirit, groan inwardly as we wait eagerly for adoption as sons, the redemption of our bodies. For in this hope we were saved. Now hope that is seen is not hope. For who hopes for what he sees? But if we hope for what we do not see, we wait for it with patience. (Romans 8:18-25)

To think, for some people the "hereafter" is a harp and a halo on a cloud, or a spirit existence like a ghost, or one living on in the memory of those who knew him, or reincarnation, or ? ? ?...

The future for every believer in Jesus is glorious and substantial and of enormous proportions. Scoffers question, "Isn't this just pie-in-the-sky?" C. S. Lewis aptly replied, "Ah, but there *is* Pie in the Sky."

It would be good to remember that eternity for the believer is going to be better than anything we could even imagine.

> But, as it is written, "What no eye has seen, nor ear heard, nor the heart of man imagined, what God has prepared for those who love him"— (1 Corinthians 2:9)   (cf. Isaiah 64:4; 65:17)

We can leave the details to God.

RESURRECTION LIFE AND THE BELIEVER'S REWARD

What will be valuable in the Kingdom and beyond? Gold? (The streets will be paved with it!) Diamonds? Cash? An impressive portfolio of stocks and bonds?

Friendly Fire

When I was a youth, we sang a chorus about "mansions just over the hilltop." Does that suggest a position of high status? Of what value will any of these things have in God's future for his children?

In the fifteenth chapter of 1 Corinthians, Paul is answering questions raised by the church at Corinth regarding the resurrection of the body. He declares that Christ came forth from the grave to an actual physical life. Paul calls Jesus' resurrection "the firstfruits." That means all of the rest of us are the *harvest* and will come forth *like Christ* when He comes.

> But in fact Christ has been raised from the dead, the firstfruits of those who have fallen asleep. For as by a man came death, by a man has come also the resurrection of the dead. For as in Adam all die, so also in Christ shall all be made alive. But each in his own order: Christ the firstfruits, then at his coming those who belong to Christ. Then comes the end, when he delivers the kingdom to God the Father after destroying every rule and every authority and power. (1 Corinthians 15:20-24)

Paul now answers the specific question:

> But someone will ask, "How are the dead raised? With what kind of body do they come?" You foolish person! What you sow does not come to life unless it dies. And what you sow is not the body that is to be, but a bare kernel, perhaps of wheat or of some other grain. But God gives it a body as he has chosen, and to each kind of seed its own body. For not all flesh is the same, but there is one kind for humans, another for animals, another for birds, and another for fish. There are heavenly bodies and earthly bodies, but the glory of the heavenly is of one kind, and the glory of the earthly is of another. There is one glory of the sun, and another glory of the moon, and another glory of the stars; for star differs from star in glory. (1 Corinthians 15:35-41)

Paul is talking about the glory that is ours in the resurrection! Paul now tells us that just as beings and heavenly bodies differ in glory, the glory of our resurrection body will transcend the glory of our physical body.

> So is it with the resurrection of the dead. What is sown is perishable; what is raised is imperishable. It is sown in dishonor; it is raised in glory. It is sown in weakness; it is raised in power. It is sown a natural body; it is raised a spiritual body. If there is a natural body, there is also a spiritual body. (1 Corinthians 15:42-44)

> Paul had stated that "Star differs from star in glory." (v. 41.)

> Then the righteous will shine like the sun in the kingdom of their Father. He who has ears, let him hear. (Matthew 13:43)

There is a *glory*, each differing from the other, that relates to each resurrection body. **Could that glory be the capacity of our new body to enjoy and appreciate Jesus and His kingdom for eternity?** Consider the following:

The Apostle Paul affirms:

> ...if children, then heirs—heirs of God and fellow heirs with Christ, provided we suffer with him in order that we may also be glorified with him. For I consider that the sufferings of this present time are not worth comparing with the glory that is to be revealed to us. (Romans 8:17-18)

> And those whom he predestined he also called, and those whom he called he also justified, and those whom he justified he also glorified. (Romans 8:30)

In his letter Peter writes,

> Blessed be the God and Father of our Lord Jesus Christ! According to his great mercy, he has caused us to be born again to a living hope through the resurrection of Jesus Christ from the dead, to an inheritance that is imperishable, undefiled, and unfading, kept in heaven for you, who by God's power are being guarded

> through faith for a salvation ready to be revealed in the last time. In this you rejoice, though now for a little while, if necessary, you have been grieved by various trials, so that the tested genuineness of your faith—more precious than gold that perishes though it is tested by fire—may be found to result in praise and glory and honor at the revelation of Jesus Christ. (1 Peter 1:3-7)

Note that suffering and testing will come in order to try our faith. This faith, when proved, is valuable beyond description and will result in **glory** for us when Jesus returns.

The conclusion I draw from this teaching of both Paul and Peter is that the reward for each believer will be the capacity of each resurrection body to appreciate and enjoy Jesus and His Kingdom forever; i.e., "Glory."

COMPELLING GLORY

During the writing of this book, several good friends in fellowship with me in the ministry of the Word of God offered constructive criticism. One significant help was the question, "Bill, I wonder if this *glory* argument is compelling?" Enjoying and appreciating Jesus *seems* nebulous—insufficient to satisfy for all of eternity. I am not sure most readers would respond by saying, "Yes, that is what I long for!" This stopped me like Road-runner's nemesis Wile E. Coyote hitting a wall. The question is relevant, but perhaps some will not *get it*. But, what about *me*?

I asked myself, "Do I sense that this glory is 'compelling?'" Upon reflection, the answer came to my mind and heart. "Yes, but just in flashes." It is so limited, feeble, fleeting and earthbound, although it brings real times of indescribable joy. Something happens for good in my life and an inexpressible joy wells up *as I sense it is from God*. I am singing a song of praise to God for Calvary and for Jesus' blood and cleansing against the black

Resurrection Glory and the Believer's Reward

backdrop of my sins, failures, and weaknesses. In that worship I sense glory and gratitude, and an inexpressible joy wells up from within. I am awed at the grace that accepts me totally. When agonizing heartaches and sorrows come to me and my family, there is a peace beyond understanding which possesses and holds me completely contrary to my somewhat frenetic personality. I recognize it as Jesus and the reality of His presence. Joy unspeakable and full of glory sweeps in; I sense love flowing from Him to me, and I reflect this love back to Him and enjoy fellowship with Him. These are experiences of Jesus. Love, joy, and peace flow together. Though it is just flashes now, my appetite is whetted. I believe that the most desired moments in my life are these *flashes of glory*!

In his journal, martyred missionary Jim Eliot describes this experience:

> I walked out to the hill just now. It is exalting, delicious. To stand embraced by the shadows of a friendly tree with the wind tugging at your coattail and the heavens hailing your heart, to gaze and glory and to give oneself again to God, what more could a man ask? Oh, the fullness, pleasure, sheer excitement of knowing God on earth. I care not if I never raise my voice again for Him, if only I may love Him, please Him. Mayhap, in mercy, He shall give me a host of children that I may lead through the vast star fields to explore His delicacies whose fingers' ends set them to burning. But if not, if only I may see Him, smell His garments, and smile into my Lover's eyes, ah, then, not stars, nor children, shall matter—only Himself.[8]

---

[8] Jim Eliot, *The Journals of Jim Eliot*, entry of January 16, 1951.

Friendly Fire

Scripture does not support these experiences of *glory;* then to attribute them to God is mere superstition. However, consider the Psalmist's experience of God:

> As for me, I shall behold your face in righteousness; when I awake, I shall be satisfied with your likeness. (Psalm 17:15)

> One thing have I asked of the LORD, that will I seek after: that I may dwell in the house of the LORD all the days of my life, to gaze upon the beauty of the LORD and to inquire in his temple. (Psalm 27:4)

> You make known to me the path of life; in your presence there is fullness of joy; at your right hand are pleasures forevermore. (Psalm 16:11)

> Preserve me, O God, for in you I take refuge. I say to the LORD, "You are my Lord; I have no good apart from you." As for the saints in the land, they are the excellent ones, in whom is all my delight. (Psalm 16:1-3)

> Whom have I in heaven but you? And there is nothing on earth that I desire besides you. My flesh and my heart may fail, but God is the strength of my heart and my portion forever. (Psalm 73:25-26)

Note Jesus' prayer for us:

> Father, I desire that they also, whom you have given me, may be with me where I am, to see my glory that you have given me because you loved me before the foundation of the world. (John 17:24)

Look at the testimony of the Apostles:

> Now the Lord is the Spirit, and where the Spirit of the Lord is, there is freedom. And we all, with unveiled face, beholding the glory of the Lord, are being transformed into the same image from one degree of glory to another. For this comes from the Lord who is the Spirit. (2 Corinthians 3:17-18)

Resurrection Glory and the Believer's Reward

For God, who said, "Let light shine out of darkness," has shone in our hearts to give the light of the knowledge of the glory of God in the face of Jesus Christ. (2 Corinthians 4:6)

For this light momentary affliction is preparing for us an eternal weight of glory beyond all comparison, as we look not to the things that are seen but to the things that are unseen. For the things that are seen are transient, but the things that are unseen are eternal. (2 Corinthians 4:17-18)

so that the tested genuineness of your faith—more precious than gold that perishes though it is tested by fire—may be found to result in praise and glory and honor at the revelation of Jesus Christ. Though you have not seen him, you love him. Though you do not now see him, you believe in him and rejoice with joy that is inexpressible and filled with glory, (1 Peter 1:7-8)

THE GLORY OF LOVING JESUS

There is also the witness through the years in music and literature and of Christian experiences of the glory of loving Jesus.

> Jesus thou joy of loving hearts,
> Thou fount of life, thou light of men,
> From the best bliss that earth imparts,
> I turn unfilled to Thee again.
>   Bernard of Clairvaux

> Jesus priceless treasure,
> Source of purest pleasure,
> Truest friend to me:
> Long my heart hath panted,
> Til it well nigh fainted;
> Thirsting after Thee.
> Thine I am,
> O spotless lamb,

Friendly Fire

> I will suffer nought to hide Thee,
> Ask for nought beside Thee.
> Johann Franck

A more contemporary song of worship is this:

> Jesus, all glorious,
> Create in us a temple.
> All as living stones,
> Where You're enthroned.
> As you rose from death in power,
> So rise within our worship.
> Rise upon our praise,
> Tis the hand that saw you raised.
> Clothe us in Your glory,
> Caress us by Your grace.
>
> Oh the glory of Your presence,
> We your temple give you reverence.
> Come and rise from Your rest and
> Be blest by our praise
> As we glory in your embrace,
> As Your presence now fills this place.[9]

Finally, in his sermon "The Weight of Glory," C.S. Lewis wrote,

> If we consider the unblushing promises of reward and the staggering nature of the rewards promised in the gospels, it would seem that our Lord finds our desires for joy and pleasure not too strong, but too weak. We are half–hearted creatures, fooling about with drink and sex and ambition when infinite joy is offered us. Like an ignorant child who wants to go on making mud pies in a slum because he cannot imag-

---

[9] John Hall Records, Inc., P.O. Box 18344, Fort Worth, Texas, USA 76118.

Resurrection Glory and the Believer's Reward

ine what is meant by the offer of a holiday at the sea. We are far too easily pleased."[10]

How does one describe to another this "weight of glory?" As I sit in the midst of citrus country in my Florida study, I think, "How does an orange taste? How could I describe the taste so as to stimulate one's desire for this fruit? Well, it's sweet, somewhat acidic...wet...what else? Impossible!" To appreciate the flavor of an orange, one must taste it. Thus, the Psalmist David says,

Oh, taste and see that the LORD is good! (Psalm 34:8a)

GOD REWARDS HIS OWN

To those who experience it, this is compelling beyond anything else in life. To appreciate the *glory of God* in human experience, one must have a taste of fellowship with His beloved Son. This requires faith in His resurrection life in us, faith in His presence in us, faith in His care for us, and faith in His communicating with us.

My sheep hear my voice, and I know them, and they follow me. (John 10:27)

And without faith it is impossible to please him, for whoever would draw near to God must believe that he exists and that he rewards those who seek him. (Hebrews 11:6)

Just think, the value of *this* reward is appreciated *now* by those who enjoy and comprehend the things of the Spirit *now*. The more real His love and fellowship are to you *now*, the more valuable this future reward will seem to be. No one will be jealous of his brother/sister because each will have all the reward he is

---

[10]C.S. Lewis, *The Weight of Glory and Other Essays*, (Grand Rapids, Eerdmans, 1965), p. 1-2.

Friendly Fire

able to enjoy. It will not be the measured accomplishments of our earthly life that will be rewarded, rather the labors that result from "faith working through love" (Gal. 5:6). This addresses our *faith*. Faith sees the indescribable value of this reward **now** and says, "I'll give myself to that with great joy!"

There are those, even believers, who live for earthly "perks." Do you long for the investments and security for which so many live? Do you feel an envy of those who can vacation in great style? What can you own or do here that will not be marvelously multiplied for His children in God's future? Do you feel that you are running out of time? Remember that as the King's children, we do not live with all our eggs in this world's basket. **For those of us who know Jesus, the best is always yet to come!**

God is not being unfair when choosing His child to be a battlepoint; i.e., a point in time and space and in a person in which the enemy and his work are defeated. The Christian's triumph through the power of Jesus in him brings glory to God and ultimately glory to His loved child. First Corinthians 15, the chapter about the resurrection body and the rewards associated with it, ends with a victory shout, an admonition and a promise:

> Where, O death, is your victory? Where, O death, is your sting? The sting of death is sin, and the power of sin is the law. But thanks be to God! He gives us the victory through our Lord Jesus Christ. (1 Corinthians 15:55-57)

Remember the promise:

> For I consider that the sufferings of this present time are not worth comparing with the glory that is to be revealed to us. (Romans 8:18)

Resurrection Glory and the Believer's Reward

THE DRAMA CONTINUES

Let us again press *play* on our DVD player and get back to the drama.

Job's glorious testimony is the climax of the first act of the drama. After such a thrilling declaration of Job's confidence in God, you would think his friends would say, "Hallelujah!, God bless you, Job. We apologize for being too hard." However, human nature being what it is, they did not even "hear" him. It is an irony, both humorous and tragic, that Zophar unwittingly exposes his crassness when he says,

> Therefore my thoughts answer me, because of my haste within me. I hear censure that insults me, and out of my understanding a spirit answers me. (Job 20:2-3)

What he is saying is, "You said something that put me down. It made me angry so I quit listening to you and began thinking of a good retort." Instead of caring enough to really hear, Zophar's reply is a broken-record repetition of his earlier argument.

Job answers Zophar in chapter twenty-one. He is becoming redundant when he insists that evil people are very irreverent and get away with it. Job even says to God,

> ...Depart from us! We do not desire the knowledge of your ways. What is the Almighty, that we should serve him? And what profit do we get if we pray to him?' (Job 21:14-15)

"What would we gain?" "What good has it done me?" is Job's question, so he asks Zophar,

> How often is it that the lamp of the wicked is put out? (Job 21:17a)

> How then will you comfort me with empty nothings? There is nothing left of your answers but falsehood. (Job 21:34)

Friendly Fire

Eliphaz now chimes in sarcastically, wildly accusing Job of evil. He adds nothing new in chapter twenty-two and ends his part in the dialogue with a little "sermonette" that has some oddly modern implications.

> Agree with God, and be at peace; thereby good will come to you. (Job 22:21)

THE LEGALISM OF PROSPERITY THEOLOGY

There are segments of the Christian church today that are teaching a "prosperity theology." The advocates of this teaching use these very words of Eliphaz to advance their cause. The ground from which this teaching grows is legalism.

> Receive instruction from his mouth, and lay up his words in your heart. If you return to the Almighty you will be built up; if you remove injustice far from your tents, if you lay gold in the dust, and gold of Ophir among the stones of the torrent-bed, (Job 22:22-24)

The modern day Eliphaz picks this up almost word for word:

> For then you will delight yourself in the Almighty and lift up your face to God. You will make your prayer to him, and he will hear you, and you will pay your vows. You will decide on a matter, and it will be established for you, and light will shine on your ways. (Job 22:26-28)

"Name it and claim it."

They say, "God wants you to be happy, healthy and wealthy. If you're not, you are not right with God or you don't have sufficient faith."

By putting this teaching of Eliphaz here, God's Word clearly exposes those who would fleece rather than feed the sheep, who abuse and exploit for their own advantage rather than bless.

Resurrection Glory and the Believer's Reward

Job has strength for yet another reply. In chapter twenty-three, he replies almost as if he has become deaf to the pounding accusations of his friends. He expresses his longings:

> Oh, that I knew where I might find him, that I might come even to his seat! (Job 23:3)

The Hebrew word for dwelling is "seat"; i.e., "place of authority." The "throne of Grace" mentioned in Hebrews comes to mind.

> For we do not have a high priest who is unable to sympathize with our weaknesses, but one who in every respect has been tempted as we are, yet without sin. Let us then with confidence draw near to the throne of grace, that we may receive mercy and find grace to help in time of need. (Hebrews 4:15-16)

Worship with me here.

We have *now* that which Job is looking for. How indescribably *graced* we are to have on that throne One who is touched with the "feeling of our weaknesses," Jesus who died and whose blood makes an unencumbered way to God, Jesus who tells us to keep on coming with confidence, again and again (Greek present tense), to receive mercy and to find *grace* to help in time of need.

Job could only long for this comforter for he cannot find Him:

> I travel East looking for him—I find no one; then West, but not a trace; I go North, but he's hidden his tracks; then South, but not even a glimpse. But he knows where I am and what I've done. (Job 23:8-10a, The Message)

Job reaches beyond his transient feelings again.

> He can cross-examine me all he wants, and I'll pass the test with honors. I've followed him closely, my feet in his footprints, not once swerving from his way. I've obeyed every word he's spoken, and not just obeyed his advice—I've treasured it. (Job 23:10b-12, The Message)

Friendly Fire

Samuel Rutherford, a great Christian of a former era, wrote,

> Thank God for the furnace, the hammer and the file. The furnace of affliction melts, softens, makes us able to be formed. The hammer and anvil pound us into shape. The file bites off the rough edges. When God is finished, a gift of highest value is revealed in our lives.

A PLEA FOR AN UNDERSTANDING EAR

Chapters 24-27 are valuable for insight, but Act I of the drama is playing out. Eliphaz and Zophar are empty; Bildad has one more shot. His words add nothing new.

The student of Scripture will find interest in Job's essay on wisdom in chapter twenty-eight. In the following chapter, Job longs for the "good old days." In chapters thirty to thirty-one, Job sounds so self-righteous when he recites all of his good deeds, and we lose some respect for him. An exception is his last plea for an understanding ear.

> Oh, that I had one to hear me! (Here is my signature! Let the Almighty answer me!) Oh, that I had the indictment written by my adversary! Surely I would carry it on my shoulder; I would bind it on me as a crown; I would give him an account of all my steps; like a prince I would approach him. If my land has cried out against me and its furrows have wept together, if I have eaten its yield without payment and made its owners breathe their last, let thorns grow instead of wheat, and foul weeds instead of barley. (Job 31:35-40a)

Job longs for a writing (a *book* in KJV) for there was no *Bible* in his day. Chronologically the Book of Job is the beginning of God's revealing of Himself in writing. Remember that earlier Job longed for a *mediator*. Faith for *him* was to look forward; he could only long. Faith for *us* is to trust the accomplished work of our mediator Jesus, the Living Word, and faith for us is to praise God for and feast from the precious book, The Bible, the written Word of God!

The words of Job are ended. (Job 31:40b)

With that, the curtain falls on Act II.

Ah, modern technology. Our drama of Job began with our being seated in the theater; however, when I wanted to comment on the play, we left the theater for the recreation room and put the disc in the DVD player. Before we press "play" and resume the action, there is an issue related to the battlepoint and rewards that we must consider.

GROUP STUDY GUIDE AND PERSONAL APPLICATION

1. While Scripture does not give us an exact description of the believer's resurrection body, what *do* we know about it?

2. How are we to view our personal sufferings here on earth when compared with eternity? For what does the whole creation wait? Though we are not given an exact description of heaven nor do we know all that we will do there, of what does 1 Corinthians 2:9 assure us? How does that encourage you today?

3. Paul, writing to the Corinthians, compared the resurrection of the dead to seed time and harvest. Describe the word picture he is painting for us. What do you think Paul means when he states "star differs from star in glory?" (Consider Daniel 12:3 and Matthew 13:43 in your answer.)

Friendly Fire

4. According to Romans 8:17, our sharing in Christ's suffering also means what for our future?

5. Peter writes to the church telling of God's great mercy toward believers and the things that He gives to us. What do we receive from Christ? Why, according to 1 Peter 1:6-7, do we suffer all kinds of trials?

6. According to our text define the word *glory*. Read the words in our text spoken by the Psalmist and list ways in which he longed for and sought after the Lord. Are you able to personally identify with some of the Psalmist's desires toward God?

7. What is Jesus' prayer for His children in John 17:24? It is we who reflect His glory and have His light shining in our hearts. How valuable we are to God! Out of His love and care for us our Father allows us to experience troubles because of what those difficulties can produce in us. According to 2 Corinthians 4:17-18 and 1 Peter 1:7-8, what does trouble in our lives achieve for us?

8. This "inexpressible joy" of which the Scripture speaks is unexplainable to someone who does not know Christ. The Psalmist writes, "Taste and see that the Lord is good." Man must *experience* God. How does a person come to know and experience God (Hebrews 11:6)?

9. Christians may not have all the things that the world holds dear, but of what can we be assured since we know Jesus?

10. Is it correct to believe, as Zophar did, that by submitting ourselves to God, prosperity will certainly come to us? Support your answer.

11. Job longed to find God and to go to His dwelling. Read Hebrews 4:15-16 and explain the way in which people today are able to approach God.

Resurrection Glory and the Believer's Reward

12. Though Job could not find God, he knew that God had found him—"He knows the way I take." He believed that in the end he would "come forth as gold." What four things does Job say he has done to be obedient to God (Job 23:10b-12)? Are you able to say the same things of your own life?

13. Since Job did not have the Bible and Jesus had not yet come, faith for him was to look forward, to long for that which he would never have in his lifetime on earth. Define New Testament faith. Is that kind of faith being lived out in you?

Don's Reflections

Recently my wife and I visited Colonial Williamsburg, Virginia with three other couples. Colonial Williamsburg is one of my favorite places to visit. I love the early American history and lore, the traditions and craftsmen. One of the programs we attended was "Papa Said, Mama Said." The black actors in period dress related what slaves would talk about when they got a few days off and gathered together in the early 1700's. It was advice, proverbs, and lore that "papa and mama said."

They told the story of a mouse that lived in a farmer's house. The old farmer didn't seem to mind but his wife was not happy with a mouse in the house. So she encouraged the farmer to get a mouse trap. In those days a mouse trap was a large block of wood supported by a thin stick with a bit of bait attached, and when the mouse ate the bait, it tripped and released the block which slammed down on the mouse.

The mouse became concerned as how to deal with the danger of the mouse trap. In his concern he went out to the chicken house to talk to Mrs. Chicken and asked for advice. Mrs. Chicken said, "I have never been in Mr. Farmer's house, I have other things to worry about so don't bother me. I am not my brother's keeper!"

Friendly Fire

The mouse, still concerned, thought, "Oh, I can get some advice from Mr. Pig." He went over to the sty where Mr. Pig was wallowing in a freshly watered mud hole. "Mr. Pig, what do you advise concerning the mouse trap?" As Mr. Pig wallowed he said, "I have never been in Mr. Farmer's house, and I can't be bothered with such nonsense. I am not my brother's keeper," and he rolled over in his mud.

Still concerned, the mouse wondered who he could get advice from concerning this mouse trap. Oh, Mrs. Cow would certainly be the one. So off to the pasture he went. He traveled through tall, lush, green grass to get to Mrs. Cow, and there up on the hill stood Mrs. Cow. The mouse approached Mrs. Cow and asked, "What advice can you give regarding the trap?" Mrs. Cow responded that she had never been in Mr. Farmer's house and to moooove over because she wanted to eat the lush grass where the mouse was. The mouse pleaded, "But what should I do regarding the trap?" Mrs. Cow responded again, "It is of no concern to me. I am not my brother's keeper. Moooove over, I want to eat!"

By this time it was getting dark and the mouse headed back to the farmer's house. Being dark, the mouse was very concerned about entering the farmer's house for he didn't know where the trap would be. As he crawled up the steps he heard a loud SLAM and then footsteps coming down the stairs. It was the farmer's wife, and as she reached down to see what was trapped, a copperhead struck out and bit her on the wrist. She screamed and another set of footsteps came running down the stairs. The farmer went to tend to his wife's wound and sent for the doctor. The doctor came immediately and administered aid. In appreciation and payment for the doctor's service the farmer wanted to give him some chicken soup. So he went out to the hen house and did what he had to do to the chicken and made the soup for the doctor.

Resurrection Glory and the Believer's Reward

Unfortunately, the wife did not progress well and needed further attention. Many of the neighbors pitched in to provide help and aid. To express his appreciation the farmer wanted to treat them to some fine pork chops, bacon and pork loin. So he went out to the pig pen and did what he had to do to the pig and prepared the feast. To the farmer's dismay, his wife did not improve and she passed. Because of the farmer's generosity and fine standing, everyone in the county showed up for the funeral. To show his appreciation the farmer wanted to provide his friends with a meal of steaks, rump roast and the finest sirloin. So he went out to the pasture and did what he had to do to the cow and prepared the meal for his friends.

As the mouse pondered what he had witnessed, he became convinced that, in fact, we are our brother's keepers!

As I heard this story, I couldn't help but reflect on the three "friends" of Job and how little they actually cared about his well-being and how determined they were to preach their theology of retribution—God blesses the good and punishes the bad! They only heard what they wanted to hear and were too busy figuring out what they would say next. They were so intent on getting their point across that they didn't hear or completely ignored what the suffering Job had to say.

Friends have tremendous influence on our lives, for both good and bad. Our friends may be used, by God or Satan, to build us up or tear us down. As in Job's case, friends may be precision tools used by Satan with ingenious skill to pry open our hearts for despair and despondency. This truth is taught throughout Scripture. Solomon wrote, "A man of many companions may come to ruin, but there is a friend who sticks closer than a brother" (Prov. 18:24). We need to choose our friends wisely and carefully because when the chips are down, they will either lift us

Friendly Fire

up or tear us down. A true friend will stand with us in times of trouble and will be used by the Lord for our good.

The Bible says, "A friend loves at all times, and a brother is born for adversity" (Prov. 17:17). When walking through the fiery trials of life, a true friend will provide much relief and strength. At the same time, "Bad company ruins good morals" (1 Cor. 15:33). May God surround us with friends who, unlike Eliphaz, Bildad and Zophar, will genuinely love us and help us in our times of trial. For, in fact, we are our brother's keepers!

Far be it from me to say that you are right; till I die I will not put away my integrity from me. I hold fast my righteousness and will not let it go; my heart does not reproach me for any of my days.

Job 27:5-6

8

The Mental and Spiritual Conflict

The Key: Resisting Satan and experiencing him defeated on a daily basis is the privilege and glory of being a battlepoint.

We are aware of the contest between God and Satan that involved Job, almost to his destruction. That conflict rages today, and as "battlepoints" we are involved.

The Reality of the Enemy

Satan desires the destruction of God's people, and he works at it ceaselessly today:

Friendly Fire

> Be sober-minded; be watchful. Your adversary the devil prowls around like a roaring lion, seeking someone to devour. Resist him, firm in your faith, (1 Peter 5:8-9a)

You may need to update your idea of Satan. The devil is not a hangover from Halloween, a medieval *Mephistopheles*. He is not a sharp-featured fellow in a red suit with a pointed tail and a pitchfork. That caricature is probably *his* invention to keep us humans from taking him too seriously.

He is a mafia leader; he commands a syndicate, an army of demon soldiers. He is a living, powerful personality who works with his demon host in the mind of every human being. No one escapes, Christian or not. Because he has the lost of the world's people in his hand, he concentrates on God's people who will be battlepoints.

Those who belong to God, along with the angels, are God's team in this spiritual war. So,

> Finally, be strong in the Lord and in the strength of his might. Put on the whole armor of God, that you may be able to stand against the schemes of the devil. For we do not wrestle against flesh and blood, but against the rulers, against the authorities, against the cosmic powers over this present darkness, against the spiritual forces of evil in the heavenly places. (Ephesians 6:10-12)

Also,

> For though we walk in the flesh, we are not waging war according to the flesh. For the weapons of our warfare are not of the flesh but have divine power to destroy strongholds. We destroy arguments and every lofty opinion raised against the knowledge of God, and take every thought captive to obey Christ, (2 Corinthians 10:3-5)

The battles of this war are fought in the arena of the human mind—the thought life. Given the internet technology available

The Mental and Spiritual Conflict

for merely human communications today, it is rather simple to envision Satan's access to our minds on the supernatural level. He punches a few keys, so to speak, and he inserts anything he desires into our thought lives. Satan is called the seducer and liar; he contradicts the Word of God in our thinking and will try to convince the embattled Christian that God is either not powerful enough or does not care. He will sow doubt about God's provision and protection (see Gen.3:1-4). He traffics in lies. He is the author of the "What if" and the "Yes, but" of our emotional and spiritual struggles. He is the pressure behind our worst temptations. Because the battle is so intense, sometimes I wonder if I am not more accustomed to hearing and responding to Satan's thoughts in my mind than to Jesus'. However, resisting him and seeing him defeated on a daily basis is the privilege and glory of being a *battlepoint*.

We do not defeat Satan; rather Jesus, alive in us by the Holy Spirit, defeats him. However, there are some basic scriptural truths that help us focus on Jesus as our *mighty warrior*.

The Weapons

The Bible points out three *weapons* of our warfare:

Now the salvation and the power and the kingdom of our God and the authority of his Christ have come, for the accuser of our brothers has been thrown down, who accuses them day and night before our God. And they have conquered him by the blood of the Lamb and by the word of their testimony, for they loved not their lives even unto death. Therefore, rejoice, O heavens and you who dwell in them! (Revelation 12:10b-12a)

Note that the devil is overcome by the following:

Friendly Fire

1. The Blood of the Lamb

Personal trust in the blood shed and the life poured out by Jesus on Calvary is the bedrock of our strength. If we are not certain that Jesus' work for us on the cross, and that work alone, has satisfied our sin debt completely, we will not be able to answer the *accuser* in the mental battle.

<u>Our Death and Resurrection With Christ.</u>

We know that our old self was crucified with him in order that the body of sin might be brought to nothing, so that we would no longer be enslaved to sin. For one who has died has been set free from sin...So you also must consider yourselves dead to sin and alive to God in Christ Jesus. (Romans 6:6-7,11)

<u>Our Position in Christ.</u>

For our sake he made him to be sin who knew no sin, so that in him we might become the righteousness of God. (2 Corinthians 5:21)

There is therefore now no condemnation for those who are in Christ Jesus. (Romans 8:1)

So often in the spiritual fight, Satan assaults my mind with my failures and weaknesses. I can do nothing more than say in my soul, "Jesus, I have no hope but Your grace. I will accept nothing of Satan's trashing of me; he has no claim on me at all!" Jesus stymies the accuser, the liar.

As the drama of Job unfolds, we can see the battle raging in his mind. The lies of the enemy are relentless, the counsel of his friends would bring confusion, and his losses in the attacks would bring darkness and despair. It is only as he holds on to the glimpses of reality which God brings to him that he is able to endure.

Far be it from me to say that you are right; till I die I will not put away my integrity from me. I hold fast my righteousness and will

The Mental and Spiritual Conflict

not let it go; my heart does not reproach me for any of my days. (Job 27:5-6)

2. The Word of God to Which We Testify

Biblical truth, pointedly applied, is the only effective answer to Satan's lies. It is our weapon of both defense and offense:

> In all circumstances take up the shield of faith, with which you can extinguish all the flaming darts of the evil one; and take the helmet of salvation, and the sword of the Spirit, which is the word of God, (Ephesians 6:16-17)

Incidentally,

> So faith comes from hearing, and hearing through the word of Christ. (Romans 10:17)

Jesus Himself is our teacher and example in the use of this weapon. He said,

> If you abide in my word, you are truly my disciples, and you will know the truth, and the truth will set you free. (John 8:31b-32)

Satan came to our Savior in the desert and tempted Him:

> And Jesus, full of the Holy Spirit, returned from the Jordan and was led by the Spirit in the wilderness for forty days, being tempted by the devil. And he ate nothing during those days. And when they were ended, he was hungry. The devil said to him, "If you are the Son of God, command this stone to become bread." And Jesus answered him, "It is written, 'Man shall not live by bread alone.'" And the devil took him up and showed him all the kingdoms of the world in a moment of time, and said to him, "To you I will give all this authority and their glory, for it has been delivered to me, and I give it to whom I will. If you, then, will worship me, it will all be yours." And Jesus answered him, "It is written, 'You shall worship the Lord your God, and him only shall you serve.'" And he took him to Jerusalem and set him on

Friendly Fire

> the pinnacle of the temple and said to him, "If you are the Son of God, throw yourself down from here, for it is written, 'He will command his angels concerning you, to guard you,' and 'On their hands they will bear you up, lest you strike your foot against a stone.'" And Jesus answered him, "It is said, 'You shall not put the Lord your God to the test.'" And when the devil had ended every temptation, he departed from him until an opportune time. (Luke 4:1-13)

Luke wrote, "When the devil had ended *every* temptation." The writer of the book of Hebrews writes that Jesus was

> in every respect has been tempted as we are, yet without sin. (Hebrews 4:15b)

Satan was able to punch his thinking into Jesus' mind. Jesus did not *own* the devil's tempting but answered every thought with "It is written," the Word of God. **We can counter Satan's lies by talking God's truth to ourselves**.

3. Obedient Faith

The weapon of faith is "Lord, I trust you with my life, no matter what." Shadrach, Meshach, and Abednego model this weapon's use. Nebuchadnezzar ordered them to bow down to his image or be thrown into the fiery furnace. Their response was,

> If this be so, our God whom we serve is able to deliver us from the burning fiery furnace, and he will deliver us out of your hand, O king. But if not, be it known to you, O king, that we will not serve your gods or worship the golden image that you have set up. (Daniel 3:17-18)

This *faith* (trust unto death) is not some quality you gain by gritting your teeth and determining to have. "We love not our lives unto death" by ratifying *negatively* that we *have died in*

Christ and *are* dead to sin, and *positively* that we are *alive* in Christ and *He is alive in us.*

> I have been crucified with Christ. It is no longer I who live, but Christ who lives in me. And the life I now live in the flesh I live by faith in the Son of God, who loved me and gave himself for me. (Galatians 2:20)

> So the result is that to His own,

> To them God chose to make known how great among the Gentiles are the riches of the glory of this mystery, which is Christ in you, the hope of glory. (Colossians 1:27)

Not glory by and by but living gloriously now! Use this weapon. Believe that which God says about you is true. Depend on the truth of who and what you are in Jesus.

Scripture establishes that these weapons have divine power and are mighty through God. There is a glorious liberation when embattled believers *see* that it is not their fighting that wins this mental war, but it is Jesus alive in them who brings the thoughts into captivity and demolishes strongholds. Consciously turn Satan's thoughts over to Jesus and *expect* him to be delivering you.

The Strategy

In warfare it is taken for granted that good weapons are indispensable, but there is more. Unless there is a strategy for using the weapons, they lie idle. God has given a strategy for triumph. The elements of strategy against Satan's work in our minds are the following:

1. Prayer

In Ephesians, Paul introduces the fact of spiritual conflict and instructs the Christian soldiers in their armor and weaponry. He concludes with the first element of spiritual strategy:

Friendly Fire

> praying at all times in the Spirit, with all prayer and supplication. To that end keep alert with all perseverance, making supplication for all the saints, (Ephesians 6:18)

Prayer is fellowship with God, through the authority of Jesus, and by means of the indwelling Holy Spirit. It is talking to Him, listening for Him, and communication in the soul of a loved child with a loving father. When we are sure of our acceptance by Him, we run at any moment into His presence. This is not a ritual, nor is it reserved for only one period of time in a day. We are to *pray without ceasing* (1 Thess. 5:17).

For a person experiencing the pressure of being a battlepoint, the strategy of prayer is almost reflexive. When we hurt, we talk to God about it. We have no strength in ourselves or even in our prayers. Through prayer we turn the battle over to Jesus, and Satan eases off. He gets tired of getting *"beat up"* by the truth of our oneness in Christ.

2. Praise/Worship

There is so much warfare in the Old Testament that some who do not understand the symbolic significance are offended. The warfare of the Old Testament is a picture, in the physical and material world, of truth in the spiritual realm.

> Who is this King of glory? The LORD, strong and mighty, the LORD, mighty in battle! (Psalm 24:8)

> Let the high praises of God be in their throats and two-edged swords in their hands, (Psalm 149:6)

Charles H. Spurgeon affirms,

> In this Israel was not an example, but a type; we will not copy the chosen people in making literal war. But

The Mental and Spiritual Conflict

we will fulfill the emblem by carrying on spiritual war.[11]

Contemporary author Warren Wiersbe writes:

> Our spiritual praise and worship of God hinders Satan's work, defeats his plans, robs him of territory, and increases his hatred of God and God's people. So long as we do not worship God in spirit, Satan is happy to let us do anything else we want to; for he knows that all our man-made programs, no matter how seemingly successful, can never storm the gates of hell and defeat demonic armies.[12]

When the enemies of God's people came against them in the days of Jehoshaphat the King, he prayed,

> O our God, will you not execute judgment on them? For we are powerless against this great horde that is coming against us. We do not know what to do, but our eyes are on you. (2 Chronicles 20:12)

God gave him a promise through Jahaziel, a Levite:

> Do not be afraid and do not be dismayed at this great horde, for the battle is not yours but God's. (2 Chronicles 20:15b)

Therefore, Jehoshaphat

> And when he had taken counsel with the people, he appointed those who were to sing to the LORD and praise him in holy attire, as they went before the army, and say, "Give thanks to the LORD, for his steadfast love endures forever." (2 Chronicles 20:21)

Sounds like a weird way to win a war, but as they *began to sing and praise,* the Lord set ambushes against the invaders of Israel and they were defeated (2 Chr. 20:1-30).

---

[11]C.H. Spurgeon, *The Treasury of David*, Vol. 7, (Grand Rapids: Baker Book House, 1977), p. 439

[12]Warren W. Wiersbe, *Real Worship*, (Nelson, Nashville, Tennessee, 1986), p. 149.

Friendly Fire

A successful strategy against Satan's work in our minds is praise. The devil can tempt, pressure and lie to us; negative thinking can pull us down. Although we have no power over him, we can praise/worship, and the Christ in us will bring him down.

3. Faith

Faith is both a weapon and a strategy because it focuses on *Jesus*. In fact, the writer to the Hebrews referred to Jesus as "the founder and perfecter of our faith" (Heb. 12:2). He is the source of all of our faith, and He is the one who brings it to completion as well. Earlier, the writer had defined faith for us.

> Now faith is the assurance of things hoped for, the conviction of things not seen. (Hebrews 11:1)

Faith is not a mystical hope in something that may or may not be true; it is substantial and based on the evidence of the way in which God has revealed Himself in history through His Son. Faith is a rock upon which we can stand when Satan is working in our minds to wear us down or in our circumstances to destroy us.

The Apostle Peter wrote to those who had lost almost everything in the great persecutions of the early church. To lift their eyes to see God and to encourage their faith in the midst of the battles, he talked of their hope which was alive and of an imperishable inheritance which is...

> being guarded through faith for a salvation ready to be revealed in the last time. (1 Peter 1:5b)

Just as God kept Job's heart and also shielded His ancient people in the midst of their battles, so He is our protector through faith in the battles of our minds and in our circumstances.

These weapons and strategy are not some kind of *formula* that will "work." Jesus, personally and powerfully in every be-

The Mental and Spiritual Conflict

liever, is the victor. When we turn every Satanic prompting over to Him, *He works.*

I need to share a personal illustration with you. Last night as I was working on this section on *the war in the mind*, Marian was working on the word processor at the other end of our study area. I was tired. The work of writing is so slow, and my discipline is not always the best. Also, I was feeling guilty for being crabby with her. She is frustrated, too, for we seem to be so far behind. Like fumes from hell, thoughts that could mean either or both of us would quit this work drifted around in my head. I sat back in my chair and realized, "Jesus, dear Lord, how can I be so close to this truth (writing a book about it) and not recognize the enemy's work?" Would I expect to do anything that would be worth anything at all spiritually and not have Satan oppose it, in me? On one hand I know I was just worn out and frustrated, but on another level, I know that Satan was trying to cause me to give up. All I had power to do was say, "Thank you, Jesus. Take captive every negative, evil, Satanic thought. I turn this thinking over to you." Then I told Marian I was sorry, and we praised Jesus together.

Now that we have scooped up another dish of popcorn and have taken care of any other necessary business, we are ready to pick up the DVD remote control and press *play*. Isn't this so much better than that stuffy theater?

Group Study Guide and Personal Application

1. Satan is our enemy who desires our destruction. Write a description of Satan. Include ways in which Satan tries to get a foothold in our lives.

Friendly Fire

2. To what is Satan compared in 1 Peter 5:8? How can we combat his efforts according to 1 Peter 5:9 and Ephesians 6:10-11?

3. War with Satan is fought on the battleground of our minds. Explain the way in which a person can "take captive every thought and make it obedient to Christ."

4. Alone, we cannot defeat Satan. Only with Jesus in us are we able. Name three weapons we must use in our warfare against Satan.

5. Read Romans 6:6-7,11. How can a person be freed from the stronghold of sin in his life? After being freed from sin, how are we to view ourselves? Have you been freed from your sin?

6. Where can we find an answer to Satan's lies (Ephesians 6:16-17)? How did Jesus use the Word of God during His temptation in the desert?

7. What is obedient faith? What is it *not*? Tell how Shadrach, Meshach and Abednego demonstrated faith in action.

8. We may have spiritual warfare weapons at our disposal, but it is important to have a strategy to *use* them. Name three elements of strategy we must use to combat Satan's work in our minds.

9. Define prayer. In Ephesians 6:18 we find a formula for using prayer in our battle against Satan. How and when are we to pray? For whom? How often are we to pray (1 Thessalonians 5:17)?

10. By sincerely worshiping and praising God, we thwart Satan's work. What did King Jehoshaphat and his army do as they went into battle against Israel's enemy? How did God respond to their action?

11. In your own words tell what faith is. What is it *not*?

12. When Jesus is at work in us, we are empowered to turn promptings of Satan over to Him and to think on things which are

The Mental and Spiritual Conflict

true, noble, right, pure, lovely, admirable and praiseworthy (Philippians 4:8). Are you living with Jesus's power in your life today? What steps do you need to take to ensure that you are prepared for spiritual warfare?

Don's Reflections

In this chapter Pastor Bill takes us on a little detour, appropriately so, and warns us of the spiritual conflict that was raging in the heavens in Job's time and which continues today as God appoints His "battlepoints" to wage war against the adversary.

D.L. Moody is quoted as saying, "I believe Satan to exist for two reasons: first, the Bible says so; and second, I've done business with him."

An overmatched boxer was being badly beaten by his skilled opponent. Battered and bruised, he leaned over the ropes and said to his trainer, "Throw in the towel! This guy is killing me!"

The trainer replied, "Oh no, he's not. That guy is not even hitting you. He hasn't laid a glove on you!"

At that point the whipped boxer spit blood from his bruised mouth and said, "Well, you had better watch the referee. *Somebody* is sure hitting me!"

Like the bloodied boxer in this story, we, as believers, will sooner or later be struck by the blows of life. We must understand that behind the knockout punches of life is a formidable foe, a real, personal adversary known as Satan—one who is able to send us reeling. Yet in spite of what the Bible so clearly teaches, some people live as if there is no Satan. No matter what people think, the Bible teaches that Satan is alive and well on planet Earth—"Keep a cool head. Stay alert. The Devil is posed to pounce and would like nothing better than to catch you napping. Keep your guard up. You're not the only ones plunged into these hard times. It's the same with Christians all over the world. So

Friendly Fire

keep a firm grip on the faith. The suffering won't last forever" (1 Pet. 5:8-9, The Message). This adversary launches ferocious attacks against the souls of men and women.

Throughout the book I've shared various thoughts and aspects of God and how they were applied in a variety of human experiences. As we come to this place in our study, I want to share a personal example of how Sharon and I have experienced the sovereign hand of God weave His grace and love through the journey of our lives.

During my years in Industrial Management with a heavy metal machine manufacturing company, I had the privilege to be in a position where I could hire college students for their summer vacation periods. Our two oldest children, Tami and Russ, both had opportunity to work in this program but in different years. Tami worked in various office positions during her tenure and Russ worked as a maintenance laborer getting a wide variety of experience during a very hot summer.

I remember riding home after work one evening toward the end of Russ's summer work program, and I asked him, "Well, Russ, what have you learned this summer?" He responded, "Dad, one thing I learned is that I know I don't want to work in industry the rest of my life!" But then he continued, "Also, Dad, I don't see you working in industry the rest of your life!"

That was an interesting observation, because for some time I had been thinking that 25 years in one place was more than enough. I was already at that milestone.

It was early on a Thursday morning in March of 1986. I got a call from the president of our company. He asked me to come up to his office—not an unusual request—I worked closely with him. When I arrived, he asked me to have a seat. He said, "Don, I don't know how to tell you this, but we are down-sizing and no longer have need of your services." I said, "Ray, you have just made my

The Mental and Spiritual Conflict

decision a lot easier. Thank you!" He said, "What do you mean?" I then told him of my 25-year plan and that I felt God was leading me to do something else with my life. With tears in his eyes he said, "I don't ever remember anyone thanking me for letting them go!" We parted on good terms and part of my severance package included them paying for my first year's tuition at Trinity Evangelical Divinity School.

As you can surmise, I felt God was leading me to return to school—seminary—at the age of 46. Of course, my wife was devastated. She does not do well with change, but she is a godly woman and was willing, although reluctant, to follow His leading. She had worked as a teacher when we first got married enabling me to get my degree and was substituting at the time. Now after 25+ years she was willing to return to work full time while I went through seminary. What a sacrifice! I know that I have not thanked her enough for what she did!

We sold our house. Actually, Sharon sold it while I was up in Minnesota watching Russ play baseball. We bought an apartment building to help with the expenses and to cut down on the home maintenance time for me. Another sacrifice on the part of my wife. She went from a lovely single family home to being an apartment dweller. We would live there for the next 20 years.

After my first year in seminary, Moraine Valley Church asked me to come on staff as a pastor working with older adults. God was good, and He provided for our needs abundantly through this time. We still had two children at home—one high school and one college-aged.

Jill, our younger daughter didn't want to go away to school and followed in her older sister's footsteps by attending the local community college. She had already fallen for a nice young man named David, and they were planning a summer 1988 wedding.

Friendly Fire

Randy, our youngest, had two years of high school left when we moved into the apartment building. Once again, God provided abundantly for Randy to be able to attend Wheaton College with almost all of his expenses paid. If I had still been working in Industry, I don't think we would have been able to afford the expenses at Wheaton. But, being in school myself, we qualified for a lot of financial assistance and Randy secured a wonderful scholarship from the Ozinga Foundation—a local philanthropic family in the southwest suburbs of Chicago.

During the 1987-88 years of my schooling at Trinity, our church went through a devastating split. Being on the pastoral staff and supportive of our senior pastor who was being maliciously attacked, the burden of this extended assault took its toll. Many of our long-time (15-20 years) close friends and associates left with the splinter group. Oh, the agonizing times we went through wondering where God was and how could anything good come out of something so non-God honoring as what we were experiencing.

As I mentioned earlier, Jill and Dave were planning their wedding for July of 1988 when, as it turned out, all of this came thundering down. We felt devastated for this beautiful couple, because their wedding experienced the brunt. Many of our invited friends chose not to attend the wedding. Children who had grown up together and were friends all of their lives now were torn apart by adults who felt it more important to satisfy their own agendas. Where was God? Why didn't I see the workings of His hand in this?

With those that remained at Moraine—and don't misunderstand me, it was a vast majority that remained although, in the small minority that left were some key and integral people—we began to pick up the pieces and pursue what we felt God was leading us to do.

The Mental and Spiritual Conflict

Throughout all of this, I was still on track to finish my Masters of Divinity at Trinity in three years by taking anywhere from 15-17 hours per quarter. God had other plans. As I began my last quarter I ended up needing double bypass heart surgery. This required dropping out of school with one quarter to go, having the surgery and then taking time to recuperate. I re-entered Trinity the following fall quarter and spread my remaining one quarter's worth of work over an entire year. What a blessing! I could spend enough time on each course to actually learn something!

Upon graduation from Trinity in June of 1990, we remained on staff at Moraine Valley Church. The ministry was going well and God was blessing.

During 1991 God seemed to be leading us to plant a church in a small town about 70 miles south of us. We were well acquainted with a family there, our denomination was in support and Moraine was willing to sponsor and support the church plant. With all the groundwork accomplished, we began our ministry meeting in the local high school cafeteria. Our opening Sunday included people from Moraine, the Baptist General Conference and the kids' choir from Moraine led by Pastor Clem Bilhorn. With several excited families and a dedicated core group, everything seemed to be in place for a successful church plant.

Earlier I mentioned that Sharon returned to teaching. She continued as we began planting the new church. I commuted the 70-mile one-way trip during the week, and we stayed overnight at our friend's house usually on Saturday so we wouldn't have the long trek on Sunday morning.

Halfway through 1992 (our first year of the church plant), a lovely house in the neighborhood of the high school became available, and Sharon and I made an offer on it and purchased it. Our financial adviser (a Christian man at our bank) recom-

Friendly Fire

mended that we not sell the apartment building but take some equity out for the down payment on the house. This was some wise and godly counsel indeed as time would tell.

We moved south, and the timing was such that our oldest daughter, Tami, her husband, Gary and family were selling their home and needed some place to live until they secured a new home. They moved into the apartment we vacated and everything seemed to fall into place. Sharon now had the dubious honor of commuting the 140-mile round trip to maintain her teaching job. What a blessing she was during these times!

In November of 1992 I received a call from one of the leaders of our church plant. He invited me to meet with some of the leaders at one of their houses. When I entered the home, many of the church's male leaders were all seated in the living room. I was invited to take a seat. One of the leaders was an attorney. He stood up and read a prepared statement saying that due to the lack of "good chemistry" between me and this group of leaders, they no longer wanted me to be their pastor effective immediately! God was gracious in keeping my heart calm. I did not say a word. When he finished he asked if I had any comments. I asked if they had anything else to say. He responded, "no," so I politely got up and left. To this day I have not seen or heard one word from anyone involved with that church plant including the sponsoring denomination!

As I rode home, I thanked God for His leading. I wasn't sure what had just happened, but I was certainly thankful that He kept my mouth shut, and I didn't say anything that I would have later regretted.

I shared the news with Sharon that evening, and as you can imagine she was crushed again. However, as we talked through the situation and prayed we both felt a sense of relief. For some time we had both felt uncomfortable with the direction in which

The Mental and Spiritual Conflict

things were going, and God had just plucked us right out of the situation.

Well, God, now what? All the training, all the schooling, a house purchase and relocation! Thank God for the good advice of our financial counselor. We had not sold the apartment building!

We took a couple of months just to pray, reassess, reevaluate and rest. The Christmas holidays were upon us so we took the whole family to Williamsburg, Virginia for the week between Christmas and New Years. What a blessing they all were to us. At that time, three of the kids were married. Randy was engaged to Jill (who came along, too), and we only had four grandchildren. It was a manageable group of 14, and we had a wonderful time.

God provided a buyer for our house which we owned for only six months, and they offered a sum more than what we had paid. God is faithful! When we got ready to move back, Tami and Gary found the house of their dreams, and we consummated both moves almost simultaneously! We were back in our apartment, and Sharon was still teaching and not having to commute 140 miles!

With this experience under our belts, I felt led to secure a realtors' license and join a friend selling real estate until we recovered. During this time we received no support from any of the original supporting organizations. We really felt pretty much adrift at sea and on a very big ocean.

I remember talking to one pastor friend who I respect and love dearly. He was well acquainted with the situation and knew most all of the people involved. After we had talked for some time he commented with words to this effect: "Don, what made you think that you could succeed down there? These people had tried every church in the area and couldn't find a home. So out of their discontent you went down to try to pull them together. It was doomed from the get-go!" As I reflected on what he said I had to

Friendly Fire

admit that he was right. What seemed so good and what seemed so right turned out so sour. Where was God in all of this? We were not able to see God's sovereign hand because of the damages surrounding us in these days. God, and the work He was doing, was hidden from our eyes. But He was faithful to continue His good work in us and through us, and to fulfill His purpose for His glory.

I don't claim to know or understand why all of this happened, but before we left that little town, a couple that I had had the privilege of counseling with regarding their marriage stopped by to express their concern and to say goodbye. Their words touched my heart. They said that if for no other reason than the fact that I had taken time to meet with them and share God's love for them and His desire to mend their marriage—if that was the only reason we spent that year down there—it was worth it all! We hugged, and they continued on down the street arm in arm.

Behold, I waited for your words, I listened for your wise sayings, while you searched out what to say. I gave you my attention, and, behold, there was none among you who refuted Job or who answered his words.

Job 32:11-12

Act III

9

Effective Counseling

The Key: Through Christ we can become good counselors for those we love and whose lives we touch.

As the picture comes into focus, Job has turned his face to the wall. Feeling his dismissal of them, the three comforters wag their heads and shrug their shoulders in exasperation. Sometime during the dialogue, a fourth visitor has slipped into the outer edge of the group. Because he is young, he has remained on the periphery and has not spoken.

ELIHU, GOD'S SPOKESMAN

Though younger than the other men, Elihu was a man of insight and wisdom. As he listened, he became more and more frustrated. Job's self-righteous defensiveness troubled him. Anger burned in him against the three because they condemned

Friendly Fire

Job but could find no adequate answer to either his suffering or to his argument of innocence.

> So these three men ceased to answer Job, because he was righteous in his own eyes. Then Elihu the son of Barachel the Buzite, of the family of Ram, burned with anger. He burned with anger at Job because he justified himself rather than God. He burned with anger also at Job's three friends because they had found no answer, although they had declared Job to be in the wrong. (Job 32:1-3)

When Elihu begins to speak, it is as if someone has opened the window in a stuffy room; fresh air pours in. Job was acting like a cat up a tree—hurting and hostile. Every attempt to get him down pushed him farther up the tree.

A new voice is heard. We will now observe the ministry of a man who is, unself-consciously, an expert counselor. If you have ever tried to help someone who is in deep emotional pain, you know the sense of inadequacy Elihu must have felt. "Will I sound like Eliphaz, Bildad and Zophar and just add to this man's pain?"

I do not in any way lack appreciation for Christians in the counseling profession. Praise God for scripturally grounded psychiatrists, psychologists, counselors, and pastors. However, I see in the Christian community a tendency to run to a professional as soon as any emotional or relational aberration is encountered. Carl Rogers, considered the dean of American secular psychologists, wisely said, "Any time one human being gives emotional support to another, it is a psychotherapeutic situation." That means we all *can* and *need* to be good counselors. Friends, husbands, wives, moms, dads, grandparents, deacons, elders, employers, employees, teenagers and siblings can all learn through observing Elihu interact with Job as, in a negative way, we have learned from the other three friends.

Effective Counseling

As observation of the essentials from the Word of God is made of effective counseling, we may be emboldened to see that all of us can be God's instrument of healing, just as Elihu was. He did not have a degree in psychotherapy, but he knew God. He models for us the use of six ingredients of a successful counseling experience. These are all woven throughout Elihu's interaction with Job.

Remember, this drama is ancient "psychology," and it is in The Bible. Modern psychology is barely one hundred years old. What we have before us in God's Word is probably four thousand years old and comes to us with profound authority. These principles can and should be useful in counseling *ourselves*. When we sense the Spirit of God speaking truth to our hearts and when we accept His ministry, we begin to "talk truth to ourselves."

Elihu speaks and reveals the first ingredient of effective counseling.

Congruity

Definition: "Inner honesty, vulnerable transparency. A self revealing to which another will respond with like feeling. A harmony of inner feelings with external reality."

> And Elihu the son of Barachel the Buzite answered and said: "I am young in years, and you are aged; therefore I was timid and afraid to declare my opinion to you." (Job 32:6)

Elihu says, "I was shy and afraid, not daring to tell you." To pretend he had no trepidation or to hide it would be incongruent.

In contrast to Eliphaz, Bildad and Zophar, Elihu is "real." What he is saying fits what he is feeling; it also fits what Job is feeling; that is congruity.

In order to better understand the term "congruity" in the context of this Scripture, we can observe three examples:

Friendly Fire

Elihu's appropriate anger:

> He burned with anger at Job because he justified himself rather than God. He burned with anger also at Job's three friends because they had found no answer, although they had declared Job to be in the wrong. Now Elihu had waited to speak to Job because they were older than he. And when Elihu saw that there was no answer in the mouth of these three men, he burned with anger. (Job 32:2b-5)

Paul describes congruity in expressing appropriate anger:

> Be angry and do not sin; do not let the sun go down on your anger, (Ephesians 4:26)

There is no hint in Elihu or Paul that covering our anger with denial or pretense is either acceptable or effective.

A second example of congruity is

Honest confidence:

> He burned with anger at Job because he justified himself rather than God. He burned with anger also at Job's three friends because they had found no answer, although they had declared Job to be in the wrong. Now Elihu had waited to speak to Job because they were older than he. And when Elihu saw that there was no answer in the mouth of these three men, he burned with anger. (Job 32:2b-5)

Elihu did not say, "I may be wrong, but…" When this device is used, it is usually a protection. We do not really think we are wrong, but we want to protect our ego rather than risk emotional honesty. Similarly, there is the incongruent response of some pastors and Christian performers to a compliment: "Don't praise me, just praise the Lord." Not looking for points for humility, the Apostle Paul, when comparing himself with the other apostles, said, "I worked harder than any of them, though it was not I, but the grace of God that is with me" (1 Cor. 15:10). That is congruity.

Effective Counseling

A third example of congruity is

Spilled out feeling:

Elihu says,

> For I am full of words; the spirit within me constrains me. Behold, my belly is like wine that has no vent; like new wineskins ready to burst. I must speak, that I may find relief; I must open my lips and answer. (Job 32:18-20)

Sometimes we think we have to be reserved and private in order to be respected. We want to present an image, and we fear that we will lose strength or position if we share our inner feelings or show our struggles.

I am reluctant to leave this example of congruity, for it is absolutely crucial. Proverbs 27:19 states,

> As in water face *reflects* face, so a man's heart *reveals* the man. (NKJV)

> Just as water mirrors your face, so your face mirrors your heart. (The Message)

> As water reflects a face, so a man's heart reflects the man. (NIV)

We have all been in conversations in which someone shared deep hurts. Coincidentally, we have a similar problem. Our inner response is, "You too!?" An instant bond begins.

When we look in the water (mirror), we know ourselves from the image reflected. When we open our heart to others, we gain insight into our own being by that which they reflect.

This feels scary, like a big risk; people may not be open with us when we vulnerably share with them. Because of their fear of intimacy, they may even use our words against us. It is necessary to have a commitment to transparency, to be the same outside as we are *inside. If* we cannot share the honest feelings of our own

Friendly Fire

heart, others will never be able to be open with us. Sadder still, we will never know if people really love *us* or the *image* we work so hard to create, maintain and protect.

There is such freedom in not having to posture. The "open" person does not say, "I know how you feel." Instead, he shares himself.

This is being *real*. This is congruity.

Elihu also models the second ingredient of effective counseling.

Identification

Eliphaz, Bildad and Zophar stood above Job, talking down to him. Elihu stands *with* him on the same level. Elihu speaks to the three:

> Behold, I waited for your words, I listened for your wise sayings, while you searched out what to say. I gave you my attention, and, behold, there was none among you who refuted Job or who answered his words. (Job 32:11-12)

> He has not directed his words against me, and I will not answer him with your speeches. (Job 32:14)

> I will not show partiality to any man or use flattery toward any person. For I do not know how to flatter, else my Maker would soon take me away. (Job 32:21-22)

Elihu is saying, "I will be fair and not deal in half truths. I can identify with you, Job, because God is my maker as He is yours."

We often try to distance ourselves from that which is painful and ugly. Eliphaz, Bildad, and Zophar did this by elevating themselves above Job as judges, he being the accused. Elihu *enters into* Job's pain, listens carefully and actually feels some of it himself. **Identification is a ministry of an equal to an equal.** This *removes power* from the emotional equation.

Effective Counseling

Because of our sinfulness we sometimes think of God as distancing Himself from us. But no! In Christ, He draws us near to Himself, so much so that He calls us *friends*, not *servants* (John 15:15).

There is no truth dearer to the heart of a Christian than our identification with Christ: that is, we are made one with Christ so intimately that Jesus' death for sin is our death, too. His resurrection and its power over sin is ours. He, in His resurrection life, comes into our lives to live His life through us.

> I have been crucified with Christ. [Paul says in describing this identification] It is no longer I who live, but Christ who lives in me. And the life I now live in the flesh I live by faith in the Son of God, who loved me and gave himself for me. (Galatians 2:20)

God often calls us to identify with and counsel unattractive and unappreciative people. Jesus is our ultimate model. Since He is God and identifies with us in our sinfulness and lack of appreciation, can we hold ourselves aloof from the troubled and ornery people He brings into our lives? Not reasonably.

The third ingredient of effective counseling flows out of this "identification."

Acceptance

Elihu continues,

> Answer me, if you can; set your words in order before me; take your stand. Behold, I am toward God as you are; I too was pinched off from a piece of clay. (Job 33:5-6)

Job, you can argue with me. I am just like you. That is **identification.**

> Behold, no fear of me need terrify you; my pressure will not be heavy upon you. (Job 33:7)

That is **acceptance**—no guilt–pushing pressure nor manipulating.

Friendly Fire

Elihu pointedly scolds the three,

> And don't excuse yourselves by saying, "We've done our best. Now it's up to God to talk sense into him." (Job 32:13, The Message)

Elihu points out that instead of identification and acceptance from the three, Job received rejection. "Let God rout (deal with) him."

Under my breath, I have said that while counseling an especially difficult person. The hurting counselee's refusal to take "our medicine" makes us angry; so, instead of an acceptance that comes out of identification, we *turn off* to them. An astute woman once said to me, "Don't abandon me to God because *you* have run out of patience."

Most of us grew up feeling, "If I do well, I'll be loved and accepted. If I'm bad, I'll be rejected." We Christians, with our properly high moral standards, struggle over the idea of accepting a person of whom we do not approve. "Grace" teaches us to love and accept others whether or not we approve of their behavior. Because it is so natural for us to reject those whose behaviors we disapprove, the Apostle Paul urges us:

> We who are strong have an obligation to bear with the failings of the weak, and not to please ourselves...Therefore welcome one another as Christ has welcomed you, for the glory of God. (Romans 15:1,7)

God does this for us—daily and repeatedly.

The fourth ingredient of effective counseling comes out of acceptance and can be an evidence of it.

Restatement

Elihu continues,

> Surely you have spoken in my ears, and I have heard the sound of your words. You say, "I am pure, without transgression; I am

clean, and there is no iniquity in me. Behold, he finds occasions against me, he counts me as his enemy, he puts my feet in the stocks and watches all my paths." (Job 33:8-11)

Or, as The Message so aptly paraphrases:

Here's what you said. I heard you say it with my own ears. You said, "I'm pure—I've done nothing wrong. Believe me, I'm clean—my conscience is clear. But God keeps picking on me; he treats me like I'm his enemy. He's thrown me in jail; he keeps me under constant surveillance." (Job 33:8-11, The Message)

Job is thinking, "This brother has heard the worst, and he is still here. He does not have a tone of derision or sarcasm. I sense good will. Is this an indication that this fellow is really on my side or is at least impartial?"

Restatement can be an effective means of communication in difficult situations. A young mother spit out invectively against her husband and two children, "I hate them…they never do anything for me. They never say anything to me unless it is to crab and complain. They are always against me. There is never a 'thank you' for anything. I wish I was dead…I wish they were dead…and I can see in your eyes that you don't believe me…so you don't care either."

How should I reply? "You shouldn't talk like that?" or "You don't really mean all that, do you?" would only reinforce her certainty that nobody was hearing her.

She read the anger in my eyes and was lumping me with those she "hated" so. I had already given her quite a bit of time and had tried hard to understand her frustration.

The best thing I could say was, "Here's what I heard…" Because I wanted to help, I began to carefully restate, trying to be fair and not make her storming worse than it was. She fidgeted, wagged her head negatively and then, more calmly,

Friendly Fire

was able to take the *"nevers"* and the *"always"* out of her accusations.

It would be immensely beneficial if, in our family or in any other situation in which emotions are volatile, we could stop an escalating argument for a moment, like the football "time-out," and restate what we are hearing, then ask the other party to restate what is being heard.

It has been my experience that what might have become a very painful fight *can* turn into a time of mutual chuckling at ourselves and the situation.

There are some elements of restatement that are important to note. There needs to be **good will.** Elihu genuinely cared about Job, not just playing a "hard game." His interaction with Job was not a competition which he needed to win. In addition to good will, there must be ***integrity.*** A judgmental tone in a restatement can cause another to exclaim, "I didn't say it that way!" Elihu was impartial. This enabled him to use restatement effectively. He says,

> I will not show partiality to any man or use flattery toward any person. (Job 32:21)

Also,

> My words declare the uprightness of my heart, and what my lips know they speak sincerely. (Job 33:3)

When listening to a friend or loved one who is in emotional pain, it is best to **refrain from empty words,** such as "I understand." You really do not understand, nor can you understand completely. Restate what is said and let your demeanor show that you have heard and care. Keep your words few.

We discern a logical and emotional appropriateness in Elihu's demonstration of the fifth essential ingredient of good counseling.

Effective Counseling

Confrontation

> Behold, in this you are not right. I will answer you, for God is greater than man. Why do you contend against him, saying, "He will answer none of man's words"? (Job 33:12-13)

"You are not right." Why is Elihu getting away with this when Eliphaz, Bildad and Zophar could not? Elihu confronted and later corrected Job because he had earned the right to be heard. He bought the ticket, so to speak, and got on the train. He made the rough trip through congruity, identification, acceptance and restatement *before* confrontation. Because he "paid the price" of being transparent, standing with Job, and respecting but not rejecting him, Elihu was able to offer a challenge that Job accepted. Those of us who would sincerely like to be part of God's healing work often make one of two mistakes. When we seek to correct erring persons, we copy Eliphaz, Bildad and Zophar by pointing out the Scripture they are disobeying, threatening them with the consequences of their bad attitudes or behaviors, and hoping that they will make the required adjustments. We are impatient and even angry if they reject our good, wise counsel.

The other error can be to take a page from the secular psychologist's book and "feel with them," accepting them and restating what we hear from them, but *lacking the courage to confront.* Avoiding value judgments and the sharing of our discernment can be as rejecting as moralistic brow beating.

The skill of ancient Elihu is stunning by modern standards. In fact, we could say that modern counseling would do well to meet the standard of Elihu. If we lovingly accept a person, we care about what they do and are constrained by compassion to confront destructive thinking and behaviors. We can be confident in our counseling:

Friendly Fire

> All Scripture is breathed out by God and profitable for teaching, for reproof, for correction, and for training in righteousness, that the man of God may be competent, equipped for every good work. (2 Timothy 3:16-17)

There is more to be considered at this point than the best way to deal with other people. We each have ourselves. Is there a way in which we can utilize these ingredients of good counseling to "talk truth to ourselves"? Is there something that can be food for our souls? I think so.

The truth of Jesus' relating to each of His children stuns and amazes me. "*His name* is Wonderful, *Counselor,* Mighty God, Prince of Peace" (Isaiah 9:6). I may not have available a Christian psychologist, pastor or even a caring friend, but if I have Jesus, He is the one who does the healing.

There are times when a skilled Christian professional can help us. We may have a need to sort through things that seem to be hindering us from coming to Jesus for emotional heart healing. My concern, however, is the Christian community's "knee jerk" response: "Do you know a good *'shrink'*?"

There was a time when I did not realize that whatever a human counselor does for me, Jesus is giving to me personally, intimately and continually. He is congruity personified. Through Him (the living Word) and The Bible (the written Word), I have the ultimate in counseling. He walks with me every moment of my life, interacting with my thoughts, confronting, restating and instructing. As I grow in grace, my life grows richer. *He* is the supreme counselor and healer…and so available! Again, I think of the passage in Hebrews:

> For we do not have a high priest who is unable to sympathize with our weaknesses, but one who in every respect has been tempted as we are, yet without sin. Let us then with confidence

Effective Counseling

draw near to the throne of grace, that we may receive mercy and find grace to help in time of need. (Hebrews 4:15-16)

We have in Jesus the answer to Job's cry for a mediator. Christ is the High Priest who not only knows us intimately but represents us to the Father and brings to us His mercy and grace for each time of need.

Group Study Guide and Personal Application

1. Elihu came on the scene, a man who knew God and was used by God. For what two reasons was he angry with Job and Job's friends? Do you see Elihu's anger as appropriate? Support your answer.

2. Sometimes we find ourselves "beating around the bush" or being too quiet when given an opportunity to exhort a needy person. How did Elihu feel (Job 32:18-20) about the situation before him? To what conclusion did he come?

3. Can you recall a time when you opened your life to another person, shared your honest feelings, and were really able to help that friend? Did you gain any insight into your own life as Proverbs 27:19 suggests?

4. Instead of talking down to Job, Elihu stood with him. What valuable thing did Elihu do for Job in Job 32:11-12? What does Elihu promise to do in Job 32:14,21-22? How does this differ from the treatment Job received from Eliphaz, Bildad, and Zophar?

5. Elihu *identified* with Job. His empathizing created an equality between the two of them. Explain the way in which identifying with another person can put both of you on equal ground.

Friendly Fire

6. What does it mean to be identified with Christ? How can we become identified with him?

7. What should be our criteria for choosing the people we will counsel?

8. After Elihu identified with Job, what message did he convey to Job in Job 33:7? Of what does Elihu accuse Job's other three friends?

9. Have you ever found difficulty in accepting a person whose behavior you do not approve?

10. In Job 33:8-11 explain how Elihu convinces Job that he is really listening to him?

11. Explain how restating what a person has said can help him. How might you be helped by asking someone to restate your words? What three important things do we need to remember about restatement?

12. Tell how Elihu earned the right to confront Job and summarize his method of counseling.

13. Describe the two errors people frequently make when desiring to correct an erring person.

14. Who is our greatest Counselor? How does Jesus give us the best counsel available?

Don's Reflections

As we come to the end of the three rounds of arguments from Job's three "friends" and the retorts by Job, we find that his friends are furious with him and keep directing their scathing accusations his way. Rather than withholding their anger, they unloaded it on Job. Job was reeling under the onslaught of their outbursts of temper. Their anger had raised Job's anger against them and God.

Regarding anger, I think another story from an early 1700's "gathering" of a group of slaves may be appropriate.

A young man was talking to a gentleman before leaving for battle. The gentleman offered two words of advice: (1) What you see may not be what you think it is. (2) Don't act on the anger you have today. Save it for tomorrow, for tomorrow you may not need it.

The young man went off to war leaving a young wife whom he loved very much. Time went by and his heart hurt for the love he left behind. The only thing that kept him going was his love for her and his burning desire to get home to see her again.

Several years went by and the young man survived the war and was released to go home. As he traveled to his home town he knew his time of arrival was going to be late at night. He was reluctant to arrive home so late after not seeing his dear wife for so many years, and he did not want to frighten her with a late night arrival.

As he arrived in his town, he walked through the streets, and of course, no one was out at such a late hour. He walked to the house that he had shared with his wife and quietly and cautiously crept up to the window of their little one room home. As he peered through the window, he saw the lovely face of his wife lying there in the dimly lit room. She was more beautiful now than what he remembered when he left. How he longed to embrace her! But wait! As he continued to peer into that dimly lit room, beside his wife lying there on the floor was another person, a man! The young soldier became enraged. How could his wife turn to another man when he was off fighting a war? The more he thought about it the more angry he got. "I will kill him!" He reached down to find a rock or some object which he could use to

Friendly Fire

kill this person. As he was groveling around, the words of advice from the gentleman some years ago came to his mind—"Don't act on the anger you have today, save it for tomorrow, for tomorrow you may not need it." He decided to wait until morning to make his appearance at his home. When he knocked on the door and his wife opened it, she jumped to embrace him. He coolly responded, confused by her reaction. She quickly replied, "Let me introduce you to someone," as she motioned toward the door and beckoned the young boy to come out. "This is your son!" The young soldier knelt down and hugged the lad and began to weep uncontrollably as the words of the wise gentleman rang in his ear: "What you see may not be what you think it is." And, "Don't act on the anger you have today. Save it for tomorrow, for tomorrow you may not need it."

Job's anger had been kindled by his so-called friends, but Job's confidence in his God remained strong although understandably shaken. Unknown to Job, not only had he suffered tremendous loss of wealth and health, he had been bitten repeatedly by the worst serpent of all. The devil's deadly poison had been injected into his soul. Through the untruths told to him by his three friends, he had been harmed by the devil's lies. As the three friends finished their speeches, they sank their fangs deep into Job's heart. They indicted Job with long litanies of sins that Job had not committed.

The charges were not true, and they confused the issue. Job's friends could not convince him of his guilt, although they made every effort to do so. Under this heated attack, Job was beaten down, and this caused his focus to shift. Satan used these three in his relentless attempt to subvert Job's faith. The devil's poison had been injected into Job's soul by his angry counselors. I'm not sure whether Job was in any condition to be able to understand the advice of our slave friends—"What you see may not be what you think it is." And, "Don't act on the anger you have today. Save it for tomorrow, for tomorrow you may not need it." Surely Job was in need of a new friend and counselor!

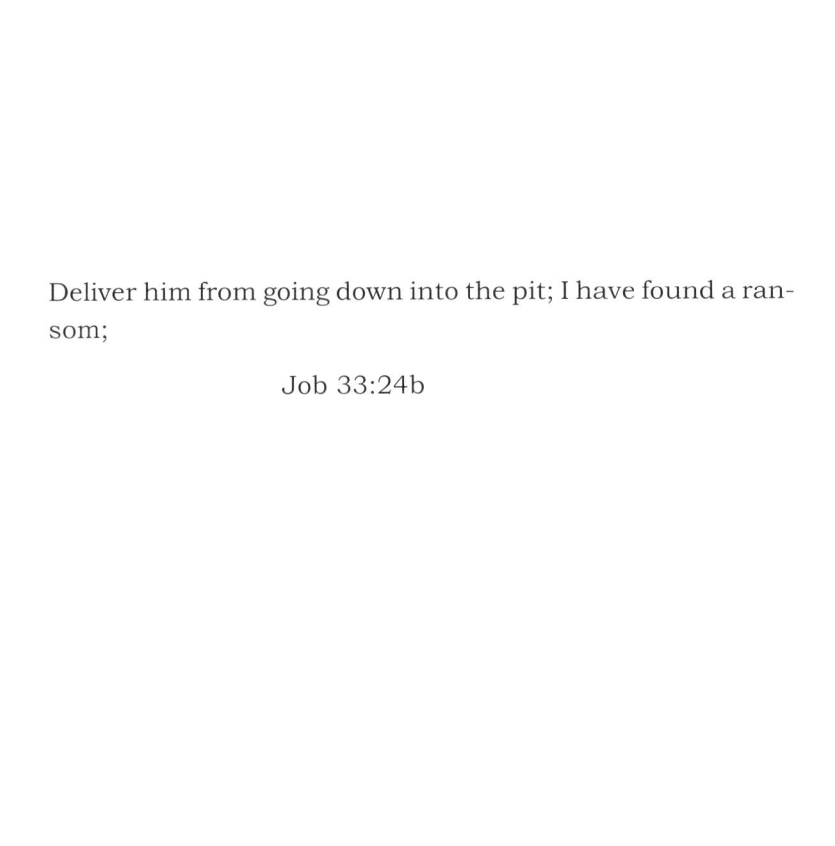

Deliver him from going down into the pit; I have found a ransom;

>Job 33:24b

10

Hope in the Redeemer

The Key: There is a knowledge of God that goes beyond mere relief. In the midst of pain there can be song because Jesus is there.

There is a sixth ingredient of effective counseling: **instruction**. Elihu fully demonstrates this in his ministry to Job, as now he moves from being only a source of counsel and encouragement to being Job's teacher. He restates what he heard of Job's complaining, and then he asks,

> Why do you contend against him, saying, "He will answer none of man's words"? (Job 33:13)

That is, "He does not answer my prayers."
"But Job," says Elihu,

Friendly Fire

> For God speaks in one way, and in two, though man does not perceive it. (Job 33:14)

GOD ANSWERS: ONE WAY OR ANOTHER

Therefore, the first word of instruction is that *God speaks in many ways*

God may not be answering where you are listening; He may not be working where you are looking. It may be that, like Job, we have an agenda that is not God's. We keep praying about our agenda, but God is waiting for us to see where He is at work. Elihu invites Job to see a bigger picture, a bigger God. (v.12)

> Behold, in this you are not right. (Job 33:12a)

This word is pertinent, for we all have needs: health, employment, family, or money. Some of these come close to breaking our hearts. Bitterness creeps in and we focus more and more on our pain and assume that He has forgotten us. However, our assurance is this:

> And we know that for those who love God all things work together for good, for those who are called according to his purpose. (Romans 8:28)

Remember the "battlepoint" truth?

GOD'S PURPOSE: DELIVERANCE

Elihu's second word of instruction is that *God's purpose in His dealing with man is to deliver him, not punish him.*

> In a dream, for instance, a vision at night, when men and women are deep in sleep, fast asleep in their beds—God opens their ears and impresses them with warnings to turn them back from something bad they're planning, from some reckless choice, and keep them from an early grave, from the river of no return. (Job 33:15-18, The Message)

Hope in the Redeemer

God's purpose in permitting trial is to save, not to destroy. Again, we can remember what Job did not know—the *battlepoint* truth.

SUFFERING IS PART OF THE HUMAN CONDITION

The third word of instruction boldly contradicts the premise of his three friends; i.e., that Job is suffering because he is sinful.

(The word *man* in vv. 14-15 and 17-19 refers not to *individuals,* but to *mankind.*)

It is *mankind* that…

> Man is also rebuked with pain on his bed and with continual strife in his bones…His flesh is so wasted away that it cannot be seen, and his bones that were not seen stick out. His soul draws near the pit, and his life to those who bring death. (Job 33:19,21-22)

The three counselors said, "Job, *you* are being punished." Elihu correctly says, "No, you are suffering as part of the human condition; sin and suffering plague the whole human race. It is the heartache of humanity, not you, personally."

This is the "different answer" that Elihu had promised. It is good for us to remember that we will not experience perfection *here,* but we will all suffer the "heartaches of humanity." Eternity is in view, and Jesus is coming to clean up the mess! That is the "blessed hope" of the believer:

> waiting for our blessed hope, the appearing of the glory of our great God and Savior Jesus Christ, (Titus 2:13)

The fourth word of instruction is, to me, one of several mountaintops of exhilaration in the study of Job.

Friendly Fire

THERE IS A REDEEMER!

I want so much to communicate the feeling and the reality of what is found here. Remember that in Elihu's day there was extant God's promise of a Savior:

To Adam, as God spoke to the Serpent:

> I will put enmity between you and the woman, and between your offspring and her offspring; he shall bruise your head, and you shall bruise his heel. (Genesis 3:15)

To Abraham:

> And I will make of you a great nation, and I will bless you and make your name great, so that you will be a blessing. I will bless those who bless you, and him who dishonors you I will curse, and in you all the families of the earth shall be blessed. (Genesis 12:2-3)

The promise was real, but it took great spiritual discernment to see its possibilities. Elihu could not identify Jesus, yet we can be thrilled at the insight God gave him to give to Job and to us.

In Job 33:22-23, Elihu claims that it is "mankind" that draws near to the pit to meet with the messengers of death. However, Job is feeling this personally! He has longed for someone who could arbitrate between himself and God (9:33), one who could put a hand on each and bring them together. It has now become a matter of life and death: *his* life and death.

> If there be for him an angel, a mediator, one of the thousand, to declare to man what is right for him, (Job 33:23)

With astonishing prophetic foresight, Elihu wards off the terror of the messengers of death. "Yet if there is an angel (a messenger from *God*) on man's side as a mediator, this is what He is like—'*One out of a thousand.*'" I think of descriptions of Jesus in the Song of Solomon, the book of Revelation, and in our hymnology.

Hope in the Redeemer

> He is the Fairest of Ten Thousand,
> The Rose of Sharon,
> The Lily of the Valley and
> The Bright and Morning star.
> One of a thousand [the unique son], to tell man what
> is right for him. [the Way, the Truth and the Life].

He will be gracious unto him and say,

> Deliver him from going down into the pit; I have found a ransom;
> (Job 33:24b)

Inspired by the Holy Spirit, Elihu could say to Job, "This is what He will be like when He comes." From our vantage point, we could say, "Job, if you trust Him, you will be delivered; the ransom will be paid. The One who will be the fulfillment of all the Old Testament sacrifices will come. The ransom is His own blood, His own life." Job was saved "on credit" (as was Abraham, who believed the Lord and He credited it to him as righteousness):

> And he believed the LORD, and he counted it to him as righteousness. (Genesis 15:6)

He could have faith that the payment would be made and it was!

UNPOLLUTED GRACE

Chuck Swindol of Dallas Theological Seminary and Jerry Bridges of The Navigators have written recently *The Grace Awakening* and *Transforming Grace*, respectively. They recognize that the emphasis on God's grace is not something new that is blowing through evangelical churches in our time, but it is as old as the book of Job. We need to be careful to keep the message of Grace unpolluted. An acceptance by God, prompted through some response of our human doing, trying or dedicating, spoils Grace.

Friendly Fire

> But if it is by grace, it is no longer on the basis of works; otherwise grace would no longer be grace. (Romans 11:6)

What insight is given to Elihu! The result of one appropriating for himself this gracious ransom is that

> let his flesh become fresh with youth; let him return to the days of his youthful vigor; (Job 33:25)

From Elihu is seen an ancient but "fresh" description of being *born again.*

Throughout the years of ministry as a pastor, many people have said to me, "I wish I could die." Although I would never reply with a smart retort, often near the end of our talk I would remind them, "Remember when we first began and you said you were so miserable that you wished to die? Let me tell you gently, I can help you out! You can die right now and be born anew. You can start all over again with Jesus."

> And you were dead in the trespasses and sins in which you once walked, following the course of this world, following the prince of the power of the air, the spirit that is now at work in the sons of disobedience—...But God, being rich in mercy, because of the great love with which he loved us, even when we were dead in our trespasses, made us alive together with Christ—by grace you have been saved— (Ephesians 2:1-2,4-5)

After the ransomed one is made new and whole,

> ...man prays to God, and he accepts him; (Job 33:26a)

Grace and acceptance are found.

> in whom we have boldness and access with confidence through our faith in him. (Ephesians 3:12)

> Let us then with confidence draw near to the throne of grace, that we may receive mercy and find grace to help in time of need. (Hebrews 4:16)

Hope in the Redeemer

It is a glorious, *ancient* truth for *today,* even for this very moment!

In that ancient day, Elihu was able to describe the promised Savior, Jesus. However, he does not stop there. He goes on to describe what happens to a person who receives this *ransom* and is delivered from going down into the pit.

> then man prays to God, and he accepts him; he sees his face with a shout of joy, and he restores to man his righteousness. (Job 33:26)

Today, we sing a worship chorus:

> Open our eyes, Lord,
> We want to see Jesus,
> To reach out and touch Him,
> To say that we love Him....

That is the experience of love and worship of the Savior by the ransomed one. Our hearts fill up; love spills over; there is intimacy now because of undeserved favor and grace. The one with new life *sees* God's face and shouts for joy!

A Life Made New

Now Elihu almost sounds like the Apostle Paul:

> he restores to man his righteousness. (Job 33:26b)

Paul writes,

> For our sake he made him to be sin who knew no sin, so that in him we might become the righteousness of God. (2 Corinthians 5:21)

Elihu has described what happens in the life of one who is made new, but he also describes what the new life person

Friendly Fire

does—he witnesses the new life to others! You can feel the enthusiasm:

> He sings before men and says: "I sinned and perverted what was right, and it was not repaid to me. He has redeemed my soul from going down into the pit, and my life shall look upon the light." (Job 33:27-28)

It rejoices the heart and strengthens faith to discover this ancient description of conversion. As forgiven sinners, we sing. If you never sang before, once you meet Jesus, you start singing even if you cannot carry a tune. Even if people try to shut you up, you sing! To the loving frustration of my long-time worship leader and associate Clem Bilhorn, I sometimes sing not only the wrong notes but even the wrong verse! However, I refuse to quit singing. The Spirit in me wants to sing. Who can stand quiet when there is such joy! Jesus gives a song.

Elihu affirms,

> Behold, God does all these things, twice, three times, with a man, to bring back his soul from the pit, that he may be lighted with the light of life. (Job 33:29-30)

I never want to get over this.

Four thousand years ago, Elihu told Job, "A Savior is coming, and this is what He's going to be like; this is what He's going to do."

In the section 33:31-33, Elihu invites Job to speak up if he has anything to say. Job is quiet now; Elihu "restates" what he heard Job say.

> For Job has said, "I am in the right, and God has taken away my right; in spite of my right I am counted a liar; my wound is incurable, though I am without transgression." What man is like Job, who drinks up scoffing like water, who travels in company with evildoers and walks with wicked men? For he has said, "It profits a man nothing that he should take delight in God." (Job 34:5-9)

Hope in the Redeemer

In the remainder of chapter thirty-four, Elihu is as hard on Job as were his three friends, but Job takes it. When one feels that he has been heard and is loved, he can take hard hits.

SONGS IN THE NIGHT

A woman in the congregation of the Moraine Valley Church attended a seminar offered for people who wanted to help others. She patted the seminar notebook and reported, "Oh Pastor, I have so many good answers." Her tone made me feel that she would not be too successful, even with "good answers." (Pardon me, but people with many "good answers" scare me!)

Elihu's fifth word of instruction keeps his promise to not answer Job's questions with the comforters' "answers."

God gives the believer "*Songs in the Night*" and it also answers Job's bitterest questions:

> What is the Almighty, that we should serve him? And what profit do we get if we pray to him? (Job 21:15)

Also,

> For he has said, "It profits a man nothing that he should take delight in God." (Job 34:9)

> What advantage have I? How am I better off than if I had sinned? (Job 35:3b)

Job was quoting ungodly people, but these were *his* questions, too.

Elihu answers,

> I will answer you and your friends with you. Look at the heavens, and see; and behold the clouds, which are higher than you. If you have sinned, what do you accomplish against him? And if your transgressions are multiplied, what do you do to him? If you are righteous, what do you give to him? Or what does he re-

Friendly Fire

> ceive from your hand? Your wickedness concerns a man like yourself, and your righteousness a son of man. (Job 35:4-8)

Elihu is saying, "Your sinning does not damage God. It may damage you, but not Him."

> Because of the multitude of oppressions people cry out; they call for help because of the arm of the mighty. (Job 35:9)

This is the "foxhole religion" of the ungodly soldier when the shelling begins. It is the "Oh my God, help!" from the godless tycoon who has been told he has terminal cancer.

These cry out to God, but none of them can say,

> Where is God my Maker, who gives songs in the night? (Job 35:10b)

"How am I better off in my misery than if I did not know God?" The answer is that for the believer there is an understanding of God, a knowledge of Him that goes beyond mere relief. In the middle of pain, there can be a song because Jesus is there. The ungodly know nothing of this.

The "little boy/girl" in each of us wants relief, *now*. Hurt, deprived, angry, we want *action*. However, the "adult" in us can wait and trust, even into eternity. But while we wait, Jesus' presence gives us *songs in the night*.

Elihu's formal instructions end. He not only gives us an excellent model of effective counseling, but his instruction is so relevant, so effective, so contemporary that we are struck by the supernaturalness and the timelessness of Scripture truth.

Remember Who God Is

In chapter thirty-six, Elihu continues to assure Job that "God is just."

Hope in the Redeemer

> I will get my knowledge from afar and ascribe righteousness to my Maker. (Job 36:3)

> He does not *bless* the wicked or forget the righteous.

> He does not keep the wicked alive, but gives the afflicted their right. He does not withdraw his eyes from the righteous, but with kings on the throne he sets them forever, and they are exalted. (Job 36:6-7)

> He also allured you out of distress into a broad place where there was no cramping, and what was set on your table was full of fatness. (Job 36:16)

Elihu challenges Job to remember who God is and to praise Him.

> Behold, God is exalted in his power; who is a teacher like him? Who has prescribed for him his way, or who can say, "You have done wrong"? Remember to extol his work, of which men have sung. All mankind has looked on it; man beholds it from afar. Behold, God is great, and we know him not; the number of his years is unsearchable. (Job 36:22-26)

In recent years in many evangelical churches, worship and praise have risen from somewhat passive participation to active, high celebration. Whatever "style" of music one prefers, our praise and worship should be out of the depths of our being. He is worthy!

> At this also my heart trembles and leaps out of its place. (Job 37:1)

> Keep listening to the thunder of his voice and the rumbling that comes from his mouth. (Job 37:2)

Elihu invites Job to hear the Lord. He takes him by the hand and leads him to worship. Something is going to happen. (The music of our drama heightens again.)

Friendly Fire

Elihu pleads,

> Hear this, O Job; stop and consider the wondrous works of God. Do you know how God lays his command upon them and causes the lightning of his cloud to shine? Do you know the balancings of the clouds, the wondrous works of him who is perfect in knowledge, you whose garments are hot when the earth is still because of the south wind? Can you, like him, spread out the skies, hard as a cast metal mirror? (Job 37:14-18)

Do you really want to stand before Him? Do you want to tell Him, "I want to talk to You!"

> Do you think I'm dumb enough to challenge God? Wouldn't that just be asking for trouble? No one in his right mind stares straight at the sun on a clear and cloudless day. As gold comes from the northern mountains, so a terrible beauty streams from God. Mighty God! Far beyond our reach! Unsurpassable in power and justice! It's unthinkable that he'd treat anyone unfairly. So bow to him in deep reverence, one and all! If you're wise, you'll most certainly worship him. (Job 37:20-24, The Message)

Are you asking to be swallowed up? God comes in splendor and in awesome majesty. He is the Almighty, beyond our reach and exalted in power, justice and great righteousness; therefore, men worship Him, esteeming Him with deep reverence.

Let the words of 38:1 shake you a bit. Elihu has led Job in worship:

> Then the LORD answered Job out of the whirlwind [of his mind?]. (Job 38:1)

A new voice is now heard. Elihu is speaking, but Job is hearing God! There is no more beautiful picture anywhere in literature or in song of God's voice coming to the heart of a man, drowning out the voice of his friend.

Hope in the Redeemer

Genuine help for the bruised, hurting, hostile person is in bringing that person into a meeting with God. As a friend, a helper, you may be speaking, but the one in need is hearing God. *That* changes lives; *He* changes lives as the only true comforter.

There are many ways of giving advice, but only one goal: to have the one we are helping lose sight of us and meet Jesus.

GROUP STUDY GUIDE AND PERSONAL APPLICATION

1. Job thought that God was purposely not answering his prayers. In your own words tell the insight given to Job by Elihu in Job 33:12,14. When you are tempted to feel that God has forgotten you and it is difficult to see His bigger plan for your life, what great truth should you remember?

2. What is God's purpose for permitting trials in a person's life?

3. Explain the meaning of "suffering as part of the human condition." How does it differ from being disciplined for a specific sin? Relate your insight to Job's situation.

4. From the dawn of mankind's life on earth, God had a plan for reconciling fallen man to Himself. What was that plan? How would you counsel Job from a New Testament perspective?

5. On what basis were people of Old Testament times reconciled to God? Read Ephesians 2:1-2,4-5. How are people reconciled to God today? Have you been reconciled to God?

6. Elihu described not only Jesus, but also the redeemed people of God. What does he say in Job 33:26?

7. People who have been given new life share their experience with others. Their hearts rejoice. What did God do for His people in Job 33:27-30 which was cause for such joy?

Friendly Fire

8. Job felt that it had not been profitable for him to keep his life pure before God. How did Elihu reply to Job in verses 35:5-8?

9. The question Job asks, "How am I better off in my misery than if I didn't know God?" is one which many of us have pondered at some time. How could you answer that question according to our text? Have you experienced a time when you were able to sing amid suffering?

10. In concluding his speech, how does Elihu try to convince Job that God is just? What else does Elihu want Job to remember?

11. Elihu desired to have Job hear God, but not in the same way as Job had requested. How did Elihu tell Job to view God in Job 37:20-24?

12. Finally, when Job was ready to hear God, He spoke to his heart. Have you sensed God speaking to you? How has it changed your life?

Don's Reflections

In these last chapters I have appreciated greatly Pastor Johnson's insightful dealing with the counseling aspect of Elihu's speeches. I believe he has picked up on the revelation that few other scholars and commentators even recognize; that is, the depth of "wisdom for the soul" inherent in Elihu's advice given some 4,000 years ago and is being "discovered" and used in counseling today.

As I have read and studied these concluding passages of Job, particularly chapters 23 and 33, my heart has become burdened with the fact that there seems to be another aspect—the "hiddenness" of God! As a result of this burden, I would like to share these additional thoughts.

Hope in the Redeemer

"Oh, that I knew where I might find him…" (23:3). Job's friends had admonished him to "agree with God" (22:21) and to "…lay up his words in your heart" (22:22). Job replied, "How can I agree with someone I cannot find?" He said, "…I have treasured the words of his mouth more than my portion of food" (23:12). Where is God? Job continues, "…I go forward, but he is not there, and backward, but I do not perceive him…" (23:8). "I do not behold him…", "…I do not see him…" (23:9). The Message paraphrases these verses, "I travel East looking for him—I find no one; then West, but not a trace; I go North, but he's hidden his tracks; then South, but not even a glimpse."

Oh, dear friends, isn't this the experience of every child of God at some time? We pray but does God immediately answer our prayers? We cry out to God, but does God always make Himself known? An awareness of God may not always be available to man. The prophet Isaiah writes, "Truly, you are a God who hides yourself" (45:15). But Isaiah goes on in 55:6 to exhort, "Seek the Lord while he may be found; call upon him while he is near."

Isn't the anguish of 23:3, "Oh, that I knew where I might find him," the cry of every believer as we grope for God in our despair and loneliness? The "hiddenness" of God—or his seeming unavailability—was a major factor in Job's frustration and likewise in ours today!

Russ, our son who is a pastor in Minnesota, and his family were visiting us at Christmastime 2007. On Christmas morning Russ got a call regarding the death of one of their cherished members, Angel Johnson. The following is Russ's sermon on the Sunday after Angel's funeral:

> For those of you who have not participated with us to the fullest degree for the past few months, maybe kind of in and out and only catching bits and pieces,

Friendly Fire

we have been on a journey together as the Body of Christ here in Christ Life Church. I would say it has been one of the most intense journeys I have ever been on as a pastor. And to a large degree as I've mentioned to you, I've been a participant just walking along with you and with the Johnsons. God chose the Johnsons and chose us as a congregation and has used us all mightily along the way.

We went through an experience that was unique, and along the way we had lots of high moments where God moved, and maybe even the culmination of the high moments was at the funeral service when Angel's brother came to know Jesus as his Savior! That had been a passion and a burden for Angel for years and it came to fruition—that's a high moment not to be missed, not to be belittled in any fashion. Pastor Tim estimated that perhaps another 35 people had prayed a prayer to receive Jesus—that's a high moment, it really is!

And along the way we experienced some discouraging moments, too. Moments where it appeared that what God was speaking, what He was sharing, wasn't living up with what we were experiencing, especially in regards to Angel's healing. And so as we come out the other side of this, I used the analogy back months ago, that God is calling us to step out onto a limb together as a congregation to trust Him. To walk with him by faith, and as you get out to the end of the limb, there are really only two options—either God, you help, you intervene, or, God, this limb is going to break and then we are going to need you even more.

To a large degree, back on Christmas morning, for some of us, it felt like that limb broke. And it has felt in a very real way that I have been, some of us have been, in a free fall. It doesn't negate the power of God or the love of God or the capabilities of God. It does

Hope in the Redeemer

not bring into question whether or not he will supply our need in any fashion. Forgive me if those of you who have been around me have gleaned that from me. I am in no way doubting God and His provision and His strength. But I am largely confused. And I think Jacob can attest to that as well. You know what? It's a reality! It's life!

In the book *The Velveteen Rabbit* it is written, "The skin horse had lived longer in the nursery than any of the others. He was so old that his brown coat was bald in patches and showed the seams underneath. And most of the hairs in his tail had been pulled out and used to string bead necklaces. He was wise for he had seen a long succession of mechanical toys arrive to boast and swagger and by and by break their main springs and pass away. And he knew that they were only toys and would never turn into anything else. For nursery magic is very strange and wonderful and only those play things that are old and wise and experienced, like the skin horse, understand all about it.

" 'What is real?' asked the Velveteen Rabbit one day when they were laying side by side near the nursery fender before Nana came to tidy the room. 'Does it mean having things buzz inside you and stick out handles?' 'Real isn't how you are made,' said the skin horse. 'It's a thing that happens to you. When a child loves you for a long, long time, not just to play with but really loves you, then you become real.' 'Does it hurt,' asked the rabbit? 'Sometimes,' said the skin horse, for he was always truthful. 'When you are real you don't mind being hurt.' 'Does it happen all at once, like being wound up,' he asked, 'or bit by bit?' 'It doesn't happen all at once,' said the skin horse. 'You become. It takes a long time. That's why it doesn't happen often to people who break easily or have sharp edges or have to be carefully kept. Generally,

Friendly Fire

by the time you are real most of your hair has been loved off and your eyes drop out and you get loose in the joints and very shabby. But these things don't matter at all. Because once you are real you can't be ugly, except to people who don't understand.' 'I suppose you are real,' said the rabbit. And then he had wished he had not said it for he thought the skin horse might be sensitive. But the skin horse only smiled. 'The boy's uncle made me real,' he said. 'That was a great many years ago. But once you are real you can't become unreal again. It lasts for always!

"The rabbit sighed. He thought it would be a long time before this magic called 'real' happened to him. He longed to become real. To know what it felt like. And yet the idea of growing shabby and losing his eyes and whiskers was rather sad. He wished that he could become real without those uncomfortable things happening to him."

I know there are a few of us here this morning that wish we could become real without these uncomfortable things happening to us. And I guess if God is calling us and challenging us and changing us, it would be to become "real."

You see, there is a real world out there with real hurting people with real pain and real confusion and real questions and real doubts and real anger. And largely the church of Jesus Christ has stayed "holed up" in our comfortable, little, not so real worlds. And what He is calling us to do and to become is a real church, real people who aren't afraid and who are equipped to step outside the bubble and to minister to real people.

There is a great picture in Acts 7. From a worldly standpoint and from the early church's standpoint, they lost a huge battle on that day. Stephen was stoned! One of their seven deacons was stoned.

Hope in the Redeemer

That's huge! What a huge loss to the early church. And yet as you look at the aftermath of that *incident*, it was probably the greatest event in all of history that caused the gospel to expand throughout the then known world and to us today! The battle was lost as far as the early church was concerned and as far as that team of deacons was concerned. However, on that day, in that event, there is a very powerful picture. As Stephen is about ready to be stoned, and as he is crying on behalf of the people, he looks up into heaven and sees the glory of God. Very specifically, he sees Jesus standing at the right hand of His Father. All the way through Scripture, whenever Jesus is pictured as being at the right hand of the Father, He is sitting. He is seated. He is ruling from that seat, that throne of power.

Jesus, on that day when His servant Stephen was stoned, stood! And, if nothing else, it communicated to Stephen, "Stephen, I'm with you! Stephen, I groan for you! Stephen, I hurt for you. But Stephen, there's a bigger picture. There's more. And what you are going through, even though you don't understand it, is going to result in huge stuff!"

Don't confuse this event and our experience with the heart of our Father. He loves us, and he loves Jacob. He has a tear bottle that is filling up for Jacob and Isaac and Cody and the family. As Angel was being taken from them, He stood. Jesus stood on behalf of that family. If only to communicate nothing else, except, "Jacob, I love you. I'm with you. I ache for you. There is a greater good even though we can't see it—even though you can't see it now!"

When I listened to this message from our son, I was reminded of our God who is often hidden from our eyes because of the pain we bear. But God uses that pain in His process of making us

Friendly Fire

"real." May we encourage each other day after day to keep seeking the God who is willing to be found by us and who relentlessly conforms us to the image of His Son.

The omnipresence of God is one of the most basic truths of theology. The Bible clearly teaches that there is no place where God is not present. This is a foundational truth that we as believers often forget, and Job certainly seems to have forgotten. He claimed not to be able to find God in order to present his case before Him. It may be that Job could not find God because he was looking for him in the wrong places or with the wrong attitude. Man does not have access to any technique by which God can be summoned and compelled to appear. If that were true, God would not be God!

We need not be terrified by the "hiddenness" of God for there is the flip-side to this coin. While God may seem hidden to us, he is all the while seeking man, revealing Himself in a thousand ways. Job did not have access to the revealed knowledge of Christ, but we do. In Christ, the search for God is completed. In His Son, the God who hides Himself revealed Himself clearly, unmistakably. God is not hidden. God is just. God is sovereign. God is always near even when He seems to hide His face.

I had heard of you by the hearing of the ear, but now my eye sees you; therefore I despise myself, and repent in dust and ashes.

                Job 42:5-6

Act IV

11

Job Meets God

The Key: Repentance is a change at the deepest core of the human heart and soul. It is the result of an experience of grace.

It was not that Elihu was such an "expert" counselor. He talked too much and hit too hard, but he succeeded. He listened to Eliphaz, Bildad and Zophar. He bit his tongue through all the guilt pushing, sermonizing, over-simplifying and manipulating. *Their* answer to Job's question, "Why has God made *me* His target?" was "Because of your sins."

Elihu put himself in Job's place. Transparent and accepting, he took Job by the hand and restated what he had heard. He confronted and instructed. The high moment came when his voice became lost in the voice of God. Job heard God (chapters 38-39).

Friendly Fire

When first reading this account, I wondered where God was going with such "getting big" with Job. But it carries a tender yet powerful description of God's dealing with His loved child.

> Who is this that darkens counsel by words without knowledge? (Job 38:2)

That is, "Job, why are you using your ignorance to deny knowledge of my care for you!"

> Dress for action like a man; I will question you, and you make it known to me. (Job 38:3)

> Where were you when I laid the foundation of the earth? Tell me, if you have understanding. Who determined its measurements—surely you know! (Job 38:4-5a)

What sweet sarcasm!

> Or who shut in the sea with doors when it burst out from the womb...and said, "Thus far shall you come, and no farther, and here shall your proud waves be stayed"? (Job 38:8,11)

> Have you commanded the morning since your days began, and caused the dawn to know its place, that it might take hold of the skirts of the earth, (Job 38:12-13a)

> Have you entered into the springs of the sea, or walked in the recesses of the deep? (Job 38:16)

These are such powerful descriptions of God's awesome power!

GOD'S WONDERS OF LIFE

When I was a youth, I was strongly impressed by the teaching of a Moody Institute of Science film *The Voice of the Deep*. It went from the minute, the microscopic, to the huge undersea mountains that revealed the magnificence of God's provisions for life in the

Job Meets God

cycles of the sea. Job was written in the prescientific era. Man's discovery of the wonders of life under the surface of the seas is relatively modern.

> Where is the way to the dwelling of light, and where is the place of darkness, that you may take it to its territory and that you may discern the paths to its home? You know, for you were born then, and the number of your days is great! (Job 38:19-21)
>
> Can you bind the chains of the Pleiades or loose the cords of Orion? Can you lead forth the Mazzaroth in their season, or can you guide the Bear with its children? (Job 38:31-32)
>
> Who has put wisdom in the inward parts or given understanding to the mind? (Job 38:36)

Who put wisdom in man's inner being, Job, so that one can counsel another?

You question my care, Job? Let me ask you,

> Can you hunt the prey for the lion, or satisfy the appetite of the young lions, when they crouch in their dens or lie in wait in their thicket? Who provides for the raven its prey, when its young ones cry to God for help, and wander about for lack of food? (Job 38:39-41)

Do you manage this, Job?

> Who has let the wild donkey go free? Who has loosed the bonds of the swift donkey, (Job 39:5)

Who takes care of him? Would the ox serve you if I did not make him that way?

> Is the wild ox willing to serve you? Will he spend the night at your manger? Can you bind him in the furrow with ropes, or will he harrow the valleys after you? Will you depend on him because his strength is great, and will you leave to him your labor? Do

Friendly Fire

> you have faith in him that he will return your grain and gather it to your threshing floor? (Job 39:9-12)

The stupid ostrich seems to do everything wrong, yet she outruns the horse and rider.

> The wings of the ostrich wave proudly, but are they the pinions and plumage of love? For she leaves her eggs to the earth and lets them be warmed on the ground, forgetting that a foot may crush them and that the wild beast may trample them. She deals cruelly with her young, as if they were not hers; though her labor be in vain, yet she has no fear, because God has made her forget wisdom and given her no share in understanding. When she rouses herself to flee, she laughs at the horse and his rider. (Job 39:13-18)

Speaking of the horse, Job,

> Do you give the horse his might? Do you clothe his neck with a mane? (Job 39:19)

Do I, who orders the ways of all my creation, not care for you, Job? Impossible!

> Is it by your understanding that the hawk soars and spreads his wings toward the south? Is it at your command that the eagle mounts up and makes his nest on high? On the rock he dwells and makes his home, on the rocky crag and stronghold. From there he spies out the prey; his eyes behold it from far away. His young ones suck up blood, and where the slain are, there is he. (Job 39:26-30)

GOD WRESTLES WITH JOB

God continues to question Job.

> Shall a faultfinder contend with the Almighty? He who argues with God, let him answer it. (Job 40:2)

Job Meets God

Job answers and he sounds appropriately humble. We might say, "Cheers, Job is coming through!" He answers.

> Behold, I am of small account; what shall I answer you? I lay my hand on my mouth. I have spoken once, and I will not answer; twice, but I will proceed no further. (Job 40:4-5)

He spoke many more times than twice. Is Job just embarrassed and trying to minimize his complaints?

He is embarrassed and humbled but not *broken*. He is not "to the end of himself," so God begins all over again. (Reader, do not miss the importance of this.) Job 40:6-7 is an exact repeat of 38:1-3:

> Then the LORD answered Job out of the whirlwind and said: "Dress for action like a man; I will question you, and you make it known to me." (Job 40:6-7)

God is wrestling with Job as He did with Jacob at Peniel. Jacob needed to come to the "end of himself" in brokenness, but he is not there yet. God is saying to Job, "You do not understand me. This power display, this flexing of muscles is not to shut you up. I do not need you, but I am wrestling with you because I love you. I am contending with you until you see that your own right hand cannot save."

> Will you even put me in the wrong? Will you condemn me that you may be in the right? Have you an arm like God, and can you thunder with a voice like his? Adorn yourself with majesty and dignity; clothe yourself with glory and splendor. Pour out the overflowings of your anger, and look on everyone who is proud and abase him. Look on everyone who is proud and bring him low and tread down the wicked where they stand. Hide them all in the dust together; bind their faces in the world below. Then will I also acknowledge to you that your own right hand can save you. (Job 40:8-14)

Friendly Fire

To *see* that nothing in *our own right hand* (i.e., our human strength of will, purpose, dedication, ability, etc.) can save or help us is God's definition of "brokenness."

Thus, in chapter forty-one, God again describes His mighty power and His ability to provide. It is a *second* chance for Job, giving him time to contemplate, "Why was my first 'confession' not acceptable?" God is demonstrating that He is not satisfied with unbroken submission to silence, but He wants Job to know His loving care for him, personally.

Job's Repentance and Recovery

Now comes the final climax to the drama as Job replies in chapter forty-two. Something wonderful happens.

> I know that you can do all things, and that no purpose of yours can be thwarted. "Who is this that hides counsel without knowledge?" Therefore I have uttered what I did not understand, things too wonderful for me, which I did not know. "Hear, and I will speak; I will question you, and you make it known to me." I had heard of you by the hearing of the ear, but now my eye sees you; therefore I despise myself, and repent in dust and ashes. (Job 42:2-6)

"Seeing God" is a biblical way of expressing the heart experience that Paul desired for all Christians when he wrote to the saints at Ephesus. He prayed that

> having the eyes of your hearts enlightened, that you may know what is the hope to which he has called you, what are the riches of his glorious inheritance in the saints, (Ephesians 1:18)

During an experience of worship, Isaiah "*saw* the Lord," and it defined his ministry. When we have a heart encounter with the living Lord Jesus, that is our experience, too.

Job Meets God

There is *brokenness* as both Isaiah and Job say, "I despise myself and repent."

Repentance is a change of heart at the deepest core of the human soul; it is the result of an experience of God's grace. Out of his broken helplessness Job was able to *see and appreciate* "grace," and so it is with us.

We need to remember that Job still has no complete answer to the *why* of his suffering, but now he can accept it. He no longer needs to know **why**, because now he knows **who**. In our human nature we want the answers to all our difficult questions tied up neatly in a box. Thus, we search for the *whys* and even make up answers! Is it a desire to "walk by sight"? Job's heart was opened to faith, to trust in God even without answers. He could now believe because he had experienced love and acceptance.

> therefore I despise myself, (Job 42:6a)

We see a change of heart for Job did not express repentance in order to be accepted. He experienced "brokenness and grace," *then* repentance came.

"I despise myself..."

It is hard to face one's sinful condition without hope of acceptance. However, when we know that we are loved in our worst parts, we can look at and face our sin. There is no denial, no need to run. Protests of personal righteousness are irrelevant—even crass.

"I despise myself."

This is exactly what the three friends wanted to hear although their method of scolding and threatening pushed Job farther from it. Job now says it spontaneously, from the heart. This is the result of "*seeing* grace."

Friendly Fire

TRUTH IN THE INNER PARTS

The closing movement of the drama of Job is both humorous and instructive (42:7-17). God has words for the three. He directs them to Eliphaz who seemed to be the most responsible of the group.

> My anger burns against you and against your two friends, for you have not spoken of me what is right, as my servant Job has. (Job 42:7b)

When we consider all the *right* sounding things the three have said and all the *wrong* sounding things Job has said, we conclude that there is much more to our relationship with God than *saying* and *doing* "right things." Truly, God does "look on the heart" and "delight in truth in the inward being" (Psalm 51:6).

Job did not have to wait for the resurrection for a happy ending. At God's insistence, the three came to Job and asked forgiveness. When forgiveness is given to us, as it was to Job (and even for offenses greater than those against Job), the forgiveness flows smoothly. When we have *been* "graced," we give "grace."

The Lord healed Job and made him twice as prosperous as he had been before. When his extended family came together for a celebrative dinner, he had ten more children, including three beautiful daughters. Although nothing is said of Mrs. Job, those ten children would indicate that she, too, was enjoying God's grace.

"Why do bad things happen to good people?" The answer at the end of Job is, "Justice will ultimately prevail. God will right the wrongs." God physically and materially restored Job's losses.

This restoration for Job is a temporal example of "suffering made right." However, for many people this does not come until eternity. Because it will come, we trust Him.

Job Meets God

GROUP STUDY GUIDE AND PERSONAL APPLICATION

1. God began dealing with Job and making inquiries of him. Summarize the questions God asked Job.

2. What do we learn about God from the things He asked Job?

3. God pointed out earth's vast expanses to Job. Why do you suppose He did this? From chapters 38 and 39 list a variety of things God created which He wanted Job to recognize.

4. What point was God making to Job by using the animals as illustrations?

5. When it was finally Job's turn to speak, how did he answer God? Though embarrassed and humbled before God, what was missing from Job's response? After listening to Job, what did God do?

6. Though God's intent was not to quiet Job, He began to wrestle with him for God knew that Job still did not understand His message. What was the thrust of the message God was conveying to Job?

7. Write God's definition of brokenness. What does it mean to come to the place in your life realizing that nothing "from your own right hand" can save you?

8. The climax of Job's story came when Job declared that he had not only heard God but that his eyes had seen God. What did Job mean by "seeing" God? How did seeing God change Job?

9. State Paul's desire for all Christians in Ephesians 1:18.

10. Job realized his need to repent of sin. Define *repentance*. Which came first in Job's life, repentance or brokenness?

Friendly Fire

11. At the time that Job repented, did he know the reason he had to suffer? What *did* he know?

12. God confronted Job's three friends, telling them of His anger with them for not speaking rightly. What did the three do in response to God's words?

13. Job's story has a happy ending. What did God do for Job? Some people suffer and do not have a happy ending in this life. What have you learned from the book of Job which can help you in caring for hurting people?

14. Why *do* bad things happen to good people? Are you able to trust God for the outcome to your life?

Don's Reflections

In chapter 8 I related an experience of planting a church. During the months following the abrupt ending of our pastoral ministry, we either didn't go to church or we "shopped" around. We were so disheartened we tried every church in the area. We even went to Moody Church in the city of Chicago. By this time our eldest son, Russ, had graduated seminary and was pastoring a church in Iowa. Dave, Jill's husband, was also preparing himself for the ministry. As God would have it, Dave was called as a youth pastor to Grace Fellowship Church in Lansing, IL, which met in a high school cafeteria.

Sharon and I decided we would support our "sons" in their ministries. For the next ten years we attended GFC and visited Russ in his pastorates in Iowa, Michigan and Minnesota. As is all too often the case in our evangelical churches, we watched and prayed as we witnessed our sons go through some very difficult times in their pastorates.

During this time of "support" ministry we encountered a series of events that rocked our lives. On August 22, 1996, early in

Job Meets God

the evening, we got a call from our daughter Tami. She could hardly control her voice as she asked us to meet her at the hospital. Her husband, Gary, had fallen while trimming tree branches and hit his head. We rushed to the hospital and already there were family and church family and pastors. The news was not good. Gary was unconscious. Blood was oozing from his ear. Tami, Gary's mother, and I met with the doctor. He indicated surgery would have to be performed to relieve severe pressure on his brain and the hope for survival was slim!

I remember going out into the parking lot at the hospital and just crying out to God. Habakkuk's words were all that came to mind. "God, where are you? God, what are you doing? You aren't very evident around here tonight!"

Surgery was performed and for the next two days Gary lay motionless. There was no response to words or touch. People prayed continuously. Russ came in from Michigan, and I can remember him in an all-night vigil praying over Gary as he took Gary's hand in his. Russ had to leave to get back to preach on Sunday morning in his church. Other messages went out to churches all over the country via different family members and friends.

Sunday morning at about the time numerous churches were getting the word about Gary's condition and were beginning to pray, Gary responded. As the day went on he responded more both physically and verbally! Seven days from the day of the accident Gary walked out of the hospital! He has virtually no side effects except a nasty scar, a slight loss of hearing in one ear, and an occasional headache. Does God still perform miracles? Is there power in prayer? Do we, as humans, lack faith? This family would have to answer yes to all of the above! Gary is the sparkplug of our family. He is the ultimate salesman and a godly

Friendly Fire

husband, father and son. As God told Habakkuk, "…what I am going to do, you wouldn't believe even if I told you" (1:5).

We were not active participants in the incident with our next oldest child, Russ. It was a late September weekend in 2003. Russ was competing in a triathlon (swimming, biking, and running) being held in Kenosha, Wisconsin. We were unable to attend the event that weekend and did not expect to get the news and results that Russ shared with us. The following is directly from Russ: "After coming out of the water I was so cold that my extremities were barely functioning. In the ambulance, the medics got quite concerned when I stopped shaking (almost violently) before my temperature began to rise. They felt that my body was giving up the fight so they started IV's and prepared for more extreme measures. As they were frantically working, everything slowed down, and I experienced a warm peaceful sensation coming over me. There was no fear at all of the realization in my spirit that my time might have arrived. As my spirit was filling with a sense of joy and anticipation, Ann opened the ambulance door. When I saw her I became immediately aware that my time with Ann, the kids, family and ministry, was not done yet. Even then the feeling was not one of panic or desperation but responsibility. Responsibility that I willingly engaged, not to get away from death, but rather to prepare more fully for it. In many ways my experience reflected Paul's sentiment, 'If I am to live in the flesh that means fruitful labor for me. Yet which I shall choose I cannot tell. I am hard pressed between the two. My desire is to depart and be with Christ, for that is far better. But to remain in the flesh is more necessary on your account'" (Phil. 1:22-24).

Needless to say we are selfishly thankful to God that He saw fit in His wonderful grace to allow us to have our son returned on "loan" for whatever time He sees fit. Russ and Ann have since

Job Meets God

adopted three children from Ethiopia and had one more biological child for a grand total of ten beautiful children (five adopted, five natural)—how good God is!

The Easter season of 2005 once again found us seeking answers from God which we are certain we will not get this side of eternity. Our youngest child, Randy, was experiencing some aches and pains which he normally would encounter at this time of the year. Randy was the head softball coach for a very talented high school girls' team. As such, this was an active practice time and with all the rigors that go with the situation, he attributed his aches as a result of these activities. However, by the end of the week he found that he could hardly walk. He secured an appointment with his family doctor for Friday afternoon. She took blood tests and prescribed some medication to help reduce the pain and swellings and told him to call her Saturday morning to let her know how he was doing.

Saturday morning found him in worse condition than the day before. In talking with the doctor, she prescribed a different medication, but then within minutes of that call she returned another call requesting him to get right to the emergency room because she had received the results of his blood test and something was not right.

We got a call from Randy that Saturday morning asking if we could be with him at the hospital. Of course, we went over immediately and spent the rest of the day in the emergency room as doctors and nurses came in and out performing various tests and procedures.

By the end of the day Randy was admitted to the cancer section of the hospital with a preliminary diagnosis of non-Hodgkin's Lymphoma—a form of leukemia. The oncologist and blood specialist wanted to perform more tests and make other consultations before confirming their diagnosis.

Friendly Fire

After the doctors left the room we all sat there devastated. Randy, probably one of the most physically fit of all the children, how could this be? We prayed. We cried. We agonized again. I knew in my mind that God is sovereign, but why Randy? Why not me? I was soon to be sixty-five. All of our children, their spouses and all of the grandchildren that were of an age of accountability were believers. I hadn't lived a sterling perfect life and had made lots of mistakes along the way, but God, in His grace, had blessed abundantly. Why not me? Randy and Jill had three young daughters. They needed their dad! Jill and Randy grew up together through grade school and were high school sweethearts. Jill needed her husband. "Littleness," as Sharon often referred to Randy growing up in our family, was still her baby! Please, God, don't take him from us. Oh, the questions that poured forth!

Sunday morning the oncologist called us together to explain what he felt was a firm diagnosis. Randy had contracted a form of leukemia called "hairy cell." None of us had a clue as to what this was nor had we ever heard of the disease. The doctor went on to explain that it was a form of cancer that was highly treatable. In his words, "If you have to have cancer this is the best form to get." He indicated that the treatment would consist of five consecutive days of chemotherapy and then a consistent schedule of blood work-ups to check to make sure that the cancer cells were destroyed and that Randy's own system was generating new "good" blood cells.

At this writing, Easter 2008 has just passed and Randy's disease is in remission. Once again, we don't have the answers because parallel to Randy's situation were other young men who contracted diseases and didn't survive! Why does God take some and allow others to remain? We believe that He does what He does to glorify Himself. I stand with Job as he beseeched God in Chapter 13, "I will accept where I am today, but God, someday, in

Job Meets God

your grace, I would like to reserve some time with you to plead my case" (paraphrased).

As Randy walked through this time one of his favorite sayings was, "God is good,...all the time." Thank you, Lord, for your grace in allowing us a little more time with our son.

In May of 2007, Sharon and I were honored and blessed to be invited to an Older Adult Retreat sponsored by a group of churches in our area including our home church, Moraine Valley Church. I was asked to speak at a couple of sessions and so, had the opportunity to do a pilot for the seminar on Job.

We had two beautiful days at Gull Lake in Michigan. On the evening of the second day I was teaching on Job and sharing some of the life threatening events that we had experienced with three out of four of our "sons." I always carry my cell phone and during this time of sharing I could feel the vibration indicating a call. After the session concluded and Sharon and I were walking out, Sharon was saying that if Dave (the only "son" not experiencing a life threatening situation) was smart, he would get out of our family fast!

Once we were in the dining hall area, I retrieved the call and it indicated it was from Jill, our daughter in Arizona, Dave's wife. Again, through the heartbroken sobs of our daughter, she was asking us to pray for Dave. For years he suffered from kidney stones and was in the process of a series of X-rays and tests to see if some relief could be found for him. As the doctors reviewed the X-rays, one of them noticed a spot on Dave's lung. They immediately called Dave and asked him to come in for further diagnosis—immediately being the next day.

As Jill shared this, we prayed. When we hung up, Sharon and I shared this information with a few of the older adults that were still gathered for fellowship. We all prayed that God would undertake in this situation.

Friendly Fire

The next morning at our early session we shared what information we had with the whole group and also took other prayer requests from the group. We spent a time praying for each. At this writing we have been invited back to teach at the retreat in May 2008. Some of last year's participants have passed on to glory. Some are still struggling with diseases and ailments. Dave went through a long battery of tests and continues with tests on a periodic basis. He has been diagnosed with Valley Fever—a disease contracted through breathing in spores in the desert dust. He is improving but has to get proper rest and the periodic testing must continue to show a decrease in the size of the spots on his lung. Once again we praise God for his continuing protection, unfathomable love, and sovereign hand on our lives.

Dave and Jill are pastoring a church in Arizona; Russ and Ann are pastoring up in Minnesota after a stint in Iowa and Michigan. Tami and Gary still live in their dream house and attend Moraine Valley Church. They are active on boards, building committees and teaching. Randy and Jill live in the area and attend Moraine. They are also active in leadership and teaching roles. Sharon and I have sold the apartment building and have moved into a condo. Sharon retired from her teaching position. I still dabble in real estate among other things. We have returned to Moraine Valley Church. Sharon is active in women's ministry and teaching English as a second language. I do some teaching and serve on the elder board. I have recently become burdened to continue the work of Pastor Johnson in relation to the study of Job. Can we relate? I think so. Is God faithful? I believe so. Can we see the sovereign hand of God weaving throughout our life's journey? There is no doubt! In a conversation I had with Bill Mills some months ago, Bill commented, "Don, I believe your greatest years of ministry are still ahead of you." May God make it so!

Job Meets God

As with the book of Job, which is not so much a book about the life of Job as it is a book about God, so is it that our lives and our trials are not about us but about our God and how He has governed and manipulated each step of the way. This is not to say that He has not given us our freedom to make choices and some of those choices were not good choices, but God, in His grace, has always been there to "make our ways straight." God is still God. He will do as He pleases, when He pleases, with whom He pleases. He does not need to, nor will He consult with His created beings, and He will do all for His own glory and the ultimate good of His people. It is our prayer that we may be available to Him when He calls!

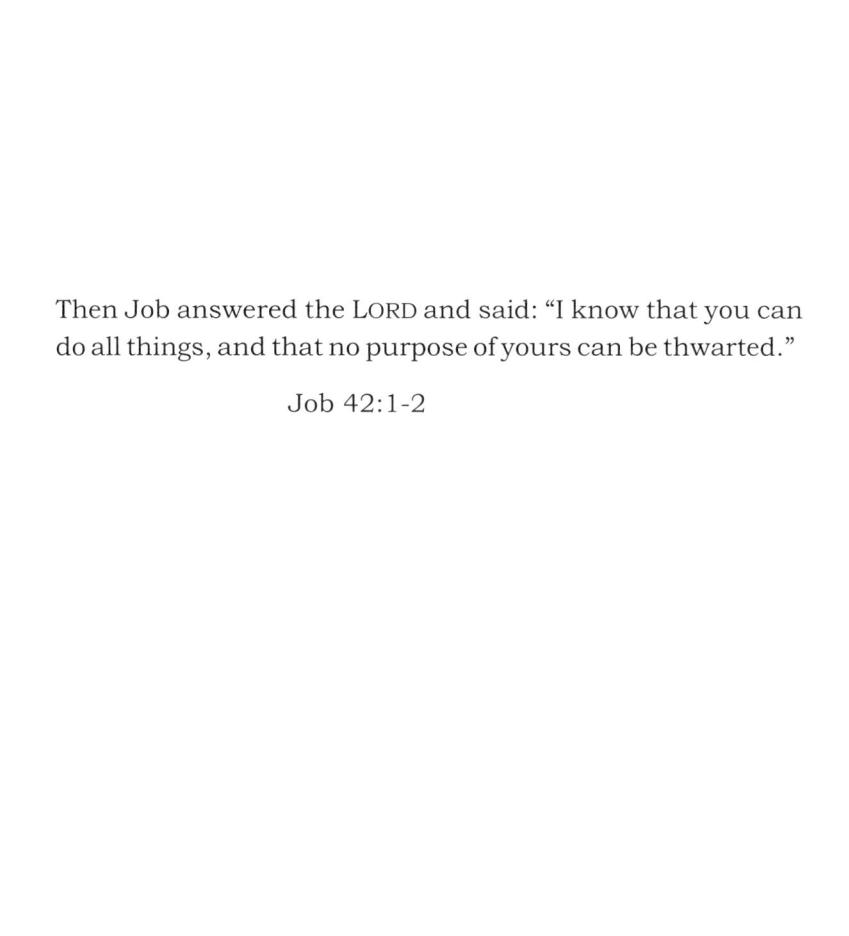

Then Job answered the LORD and said: "I know that you can do all things, and that no purpose of yours can be thwarted."

        Job 42:1-2

12

Brokenness

The Key: For God to be pleased and for one's life and behavior to be effectively changed, human "trying" must be relinquished for brokenness and faith.

In our natural human strength we want to believe that somehow and in some way, something in our "own right hand will save us." This is at the core of the unbroken spirit.

Brokenness might be defined as the attitude of mind and conviction of heart of one who has no illusions about his total poverty and powerlessness before God. He has forsaken any hope in his strength and ability, apart from Christ, to please God or to accomplish anything for Him.

As a gift of His grace, God gives some of His people an understanding of their brokenness before Him. He teaches them by His

Friendly Fire

Word and His Spirit to trust in Him alone, putting no confidence in their own efforts and performance. God may also bring them, like Job, through a "breaking process" to an awareness of their human helplessness.

Jesus said,

> Blessed are the poor in spirit, for theirs is the kingdom of heaven. (Matthew 5:3)

That is brokenness—no dependence on human strength.

> I am the vine; you are the branches. Whoever abides in me and I in him, he it is that bears much fruit, for apart from me you can do nothing. (John 15:5)

The Apostle Paul writes regarding the religious commands and teachings that depend on human will power to execute.

> These have indeed an appearance of wisdom in promoting self-made religion and asceticism and severity to the body, but they are of no value in stopping the indulgence of the flesh. (Colossians 2:23)

The New American Standard Bible reads "fleshly" indulgence. This is preferred in that the indulgence is not to be limited to sexual sin.

Both Jesus and Paul make it clear that human strength, determination, and dedication are powerless to effect a deliverance from our human predicament or a genuine change in our behaviors. Human trying has to be replaced by a brokenness relative to our natural strength and a trust in Christ for His power in us.

Our focus then shifts from our situation and the way we are dealing with it, to Him, our live-in Savior, expecting deliverance and changes in attitude and behavior from Him.

It is sometimes more difficult for Christians who have been able to put their lives together well to grasp the imperative of *brokenness.* On the other hand, those whose lives have been smashed up and have the evidence of their weakness all around them seem to embrace this truth more readily. This does not dishonor those who have their lives in order, but it does warn them that the only accomplishments in good behavior and success that honor God are those that Jesus works in them.

> For we are his workmanship, created in Christ Jesus for good works, which God prepared beforehand, that we should walk in them. (Ephesians 2:10)

This is a humbling thought.

I have known Christians who are highly accomplished and are very much *together.* They have had advantages in life and have made good use of them. They have a deep devotion to Jesus and a genuine humility that results from the certainty that God has *graced them.* Brokenness is *real* to them; they do not see themselves as above the ordinary, the mediocre. They are compassionate and forgiving because they feel deeply their own frailty, their *brokenness.*

The Apostle Paul cautions us to remember that there will not be many such Christians. He wrote to the believers in Corinth:

> For consider your calling, brothers: not many of you were wise according to worldly standards, not many were powerful, not many were of noble birth. But God chose what is foolish in the world to shame the wise; God chose what is weak in the world to shame the strong; God chose what is low and despised in the world, even things that are not, to bring to nothing things that are, so that no human being might boast in the presence of God. (1 Corinthians 1:26-29)

To better understand and identify brokenness, we will consider some comparisons and contrasts of brokenness with a self-reliant togetherness.

Friendly Fire

THE CONTINUUM OF SELF-RELIANCE AND BROKENNESS

God brings Job to brokenness in chapter 40:1-14 and in the process provides insight for us.

God challenges Job to imitate His sovereign majesty and exalted power (if he can). Then He chides Job:

> Dress for action like a man; I will question you, and you make it known to me. (Job 40:7)

Job has been doing the demanding and questioning; it is now God's turn.

> Will you even put me in the wrong? Will you condemn me that you may be in the right? (Job 40:8)

Job has contended that God is not fair, that He does not care.

> Have you an arm like God, and can you thunder with a voice like his? Adorn yourself with majesty and dignity; clothe yourself with glory and splendor. (Job 40:9-10)

When you can do this, Job,

> Then will I also acknowledge to you that your own right hand can save you. (Job 40:14)

Brokenness brings Job to confess,

> I know that you can do all things, and that no purpose of yours can be thwarted. "Who is this that hides counsel without knowledge?" (Job 42:2-3a)

"Now," asks the Lord, "who is this that denies my providential care and sovereign power?" Job answers, "It is I, Lord."

> Therefore I despise myself and repent in dust and ashes. (Job 42:6)

Brokenness

Continuum of "Togetherness" *(Self-Reliance)*	*Continuum of "Brokenness"* *(Reliance on Christ Alone)*
<u>Human Experience</u> The normative human experience is success and happiness. Hurt, pain, loss are aberrations which need to be accounted for.	<u>Human Experience</u> Brokenness and tragedy are normative to human existence; suffering, pain, unexpected trauma, and death are the basic givens of life as we know it. Joy, love, justice, and peace are aberrations* which need to be accounted for. *Note Job 5:6-7 and 19:7— Those who are (like Job) engaged in a battlepoint experience may more easily grasp this truth.
<u>God</u> God is the keeper of the "joy gate." He guarantees a certain measure of happiness and success for the faithful. He wants us to be happy and provides the righteous with gifts to keep their lives happy. He brings judgment on the unrighteous. Dark and tragic circumstances represent the absence of God. God shuns sin and chaos.	<u>God</u> God enters into the brokenness of life to be *"with us"* in our suffering and pain. God wants to lead us through brokenness into His way of healing and newness of life (Christ-generated togetherness). Dark and tragic circumstances signal the presence of God with the wounded and powerless.

Friendly Fire

The Process	The Process
Through a good heritage, education, behavior modification, methodology, goal-oriented striving and religious activity, one develops a culturally acceptable, even admirable, character and lifestyle.	Through failure, pain, disappointment and loss that strip one of the illusions of natural and cultural acceptability, one turns to Christ and experiences His gracious love and acceptance.
	This undeserved favor teaches and develops a strong faith, an inherent humility and godly lifestyle.
Ministry	Ministry
Tragic moments within the continuum of success and *togetherness* need to be fought and wrestled back into normalcy.	Be compassionate even as our Heavenly Father is compassionate.
	Be *with* the wounded and broken in their suffering as a sign of the presence of God.
Emphasize the *positive* (formulas, activities, and disciplines are instruments of recovery.)	Emphasize the reality of evil and the accompanying reality of God's presence.
Get people back into joy as soon as possible.	Weep with those who weep, and rejoice with those who rejoice.
Witness	Witness
A demonstration of the benefits of righteous living: health, wealth, success, and *having it together.*	A demonstration of the power of the life of God to bring healing and newness in the face of sin and death.
Shiny people are God's best advertisement.	Broken people who experience God's presence are salt and light.
Problems represent a lack of faith and unfaithfulness and are a betrayal of God's purposes.	Problems represent the context where God accomplishes His redemptive purposes.

Brokenness

Finally, brokenness is not the way of the world. In fact, it goes 180° from natural human thought. Without the supernaturalness of life "in Christ," it makes no sense.

> The natural person does not accept the things of the Spirit of God, for they are folly to him, and he is not able to understand them because they are spiritually discerned. (1 Corinthians 2:14)

Craig Parro, the Director of International Ministries of Leadership Resources, added this insight when he critiqued the first manuscript:

> For one who is "in Christ," brokenness does not lead to shame and self-recrimination, but to freedom. Modern psychology emphasizes uplifting and reinforcing the self. "You are somebody." "You are great" (potentially). However, they begin at the wrong place. The truth brings us to the bottom, broken— then we are elevated and "put together" by Christ.

May God give us grace to experience this brokenness and to find the source of our strength in Him alone. Then He can fulfill in us the life that not only brings glory to Him now but it will forever.

AMEN!

Friendly Fire

GROUP STUDY GUIDE AND PERSONAL APPLICATION

1. When Jesus exhorted His followers to be "poor in spirit" and also told them that apart from Him they could "do nothing," what did He mean?

2. Try as we might to depend upon our human strength, Jesus calls us to replace our trying with brokenness. How does brokenness before Him change our life's focus?

3. Why is it sometimes more difficult for "good" people, those who have it "all together" as Job did, to fully grasp the meaning of living a life of total dependence upon God?

4. According to Ephesians 2:10, for what purpose did God create us?

5. Give a description of a person whose life is characterized by brokenness. Does this picture accurately describe you?

6. When God calls people to Himself and to His service, what kind of people does He choose (1 Cor. 1:26-29)? What are His people able to do in their service to Him? Why does He choose exactly the opposite of what we would expect?

7. Describe a person who does not have the Spirit of God working in him (1 Cor. 2:14). What does inability to discern spiritually have to do with brokenness?

8. Initially, when thinking about brokenness, a person may feel that living his life in such a way would be restrictive. Truly living by this truth, however, leads to what?

9. In reflecting upon the life of Job, list ways in which you find yourself identifying with him. What hindrances do you struggle

Brokenness

with which keep you from experiencing this freedom which Christ gives?

10. If you, like Job, have relied on your own human strength to see you through the ups and downs of life, allow God today to bring you to the bottom, to the end of yourself, and then to be "put together" by Christ. Experience brokenness and enjoy freedom!

Don's Reflections

Effectively speaking, the drama of Job and our commentary ended with chapter 11 of this book. In one of Pastor Johnson's first seminars after completing *Friendly Fire*, he shared that the chapter on "Brokenness" (chap. 12) almost didn't get written. It was written as an addendum but not completed. I do not feel the need to comment on Pastor's concluding chapter, but I would like to express my and my family's immense appreciation for the blessing it was to sit under the ministry of one of the giants of the faith. Pastor Johnson not only taught brokenness but openly lived out what he taught before his congregation on a daily basis.

Isaac Newton once said, "If I have seen further it is by standing on the shoulders of giants."

If I can see further it is because I have stood on the shoulders of Pastor Johnson!

> Thus says the Lord: "Stand by the roads, and look, and ask for the ancient paths, where the good way is; and walk in it, and find rest for your souls." (Jeremiah 6:16)

Bibliography

Unless otherwise indicated Scripture quotations are taken from the *Holy Bible,* English Standard Version, copyright 2001 by Crossway Bibles, a division of Good News Publishers. All rights reserved. Used by permission.

Hulme, William E. *Dialogue in Despair.* Abingdon Press: Nashville, New York, 1968.

Lewis, C.S. *The Weight of Glory and Other Essays.* Eerdmans: Grand Rapids, 1965.

"Oregon and the Death of Dignity." *Christianity Today.* 6 February 1995: 18-19.

Piper, John. *Desiring God.* Multnomah Press: Portland, 1986.

Smith, George Adam. *Modern Criticism and the Old Testament.* A.C. Armstrong and Son: New York, 1901.

Wiersbe, Warren W. *Real Worship.* Oliver Nelson: Nashville, 1986.

Scripture Index

GENESIS

3:2	111
3:4	111
3:5	112
3:15	190
12:2-3	190
15:6	191
39:9	113
41:44	114
50:15	115
50:18	115
50:19-21	115

EXODUS

14:1-4	116

2 CHRONICLES

20:12	155
20:15	155
20:21	155

JOB

1:1	14
1:1-5	19
1:6-7	20
1:8	18
1:8	20
1:9-12	21
1:14-16	21
1:18-19	22
1:21	22
2:3-5	23
2:6-7	23
2:9	23
2:10	24
2:11	31
2:12-13	32
3:1	32
3:3-8	33
3:11-23	33
3:26	34
4:2-5	35

Friendly Fire

JOB (cont'd)

4:6-9	35
5:8-17	38
5:18	38
5:19	39
5:20-26	39
5:27	39
6:2-3	40
6:4	40
6:4	106
6:5	41
6:8-10	41
6:14	42
6:15-17	42
6:18-20	42
6:21	42
6:24	43
6:25	43
6:26	43
6:28-29	44
7:4-7	45
7:11,16-18	45
7:20	30
7:20	45
7:20	106
8:2	54
8:3	54
8:4	54
8:5-6	57
8:7,20-21	57
9:1-3	59
9:4-10,12	60
9:16	60
9:17-18	60
9:19-20	60
9:22,24	60
9:27-31	61
9:32-33	61

JOB (cont'd)

9:34-35	62
10:1,3,16,18	66
11:3	71
11:6	72
11:11-12	72
11:13	72
11:14	72
11:15-18	72
12:2-3	73
12:5	73
12:6	73
12:7-10	74
12:17-25	74
13:1-3	70
13:1-3	74
13:4	74
13:5	75
13:5-11	75
13:13-15	78
13:15	7
13:16	78
13:24	106
14:14-15	80
14:16-17	81
15:2-3	87
15:4-6	88
15:11-13	88
15:17-35	93
16:2-6	93
16:9,12-14	94
16:9,13	106
16:19-21	94
17:1	94
19:2-3	95
19:7	86
19:7	95
19:11-12	95

Scripture Index

JOB (cont'd)

19:11-12	106
19:13-20	95
19:21-22	96
19:23-24	96
19:25	97
19:25-27	123
19:26-27	97
20:2-3	135
21:14-15	135
21:15	114
21:15	195
21:17	135
21:34	135
22:21	136
22:22-24	136
22:26-28	136
23:3	137
23:8-10	137
23:10	121
23:10	122
23:10,12	107
23:10-12	137
27:5-6	146
27:5-6	150
30:11-12	104
30:11-12	107
31:35-40	138
31:40	139
32:1-3	170
32:2-5	172
32:6	171
32:11-12	168
32:11-12	174
32:13	176
32:14	174
32:18-20	173
32:21	178

JOB (cont'd)

32:21-22	174
33:3	178
33:5-6	175
33:7	175
33:8-11	176
33:10	107
33:12	188
33:12-13	179
33:13	187
33:14	188
33:15-18	188
33:19,21-22	189
33:23	190
33:24	186
33:24	191
33:25	192
33:26	192
33:26	193
33:27-28	194
33:29-30	194
34:5-9	194
34:9	114
34:9	195
35:3	114
35:3	195
35:4-8	195
35:9	196
35:10	196
36:3	197
36:6-7	197
36:16	197
36:22-26	197
37:1	197
37:2	197
37:14-18	198
37:20-24	198
38:1	198

241

Friendly Fire

JOB (cont'd)

38:2	210
38:3	210
38:4-5	210
38:8,11	210
38:12-13	210
38:16	210
38:19-21	211
38:31-32	211
38:36	211
38:39-41	211
39:5	211
39:9-12	211
39:13-18	212
39:19	212
39:26-30	212
40:2	212
40:4-5	213
40:6-7	213
40:7	230
40:8	230
40:8-14	213
40:9-10	223
40:14	230
42:1-2	226
42:2-3	230
42:2-6	214
42:5-6	208
42:6	215
42:6	230
42:7	52
42:7	54
42:7	80
42:7	216
42:7-8	56

PSALMS

16:1-3	130

PSALMS (cont'd)

16:11	130
17:15	130
24:8	154
27:4	130
34:8	133
51:4-6	77
73:25-26	130
149:6	154

PROVERBS

24:9	78
27:19	173

JEREMIAH

6:16	235

DANIEL

3:17-18	152

HABAKKUK

1:13	77
3:16-19	77

MATTHEW

4:1-11	79
5:3	228
5:4	88
11:28	62
11:28-30	64
13:43	127

LUKE

4:1-13	151
22:31-32	109

Scripture Index

JOHN

7:37-39	64
8:31-32	151
10:27	133
14:20	63
14:21	65
15:5	58
15:5	90
15:5	228
17:24	130

ACTS

1:11	124
2:25,28	92

ROMANS

5:3-4	107
6:6-7,11	150
8:1	150
8:17-18	127
8:18	134
8:18-25	125
8:28	188
8:30	127
8:35-39	97
10:17	151
11:6	192
15:1,7	176

1 CORINTHIANS

1:26-29	229
2:9	125
2:14	233
15:20-24	126
15:35-41	126
15:42-44	127

1 CORINTHIANS (cont'd)

15:55-57	134

2 CORINTHIANS

3:17-18	130
4:4	109
4:6	131
4:17-18	131
5:21	36
5:21	150
5:21	193
10:3-5	148

GALATIANS

2:20	36
2:20	153
2:20	175
5:16-18	92
6:1-2	55

EPHESIANS

1:7-8	56
1:16-20	91
1:18	214
1:18-21	92
2:1-2	192
2:4-5	192
2:8-9	36
2:10	229
3:12	192
3:16-19	91
3:20-21	93
4:26	172
6:10-12	110
6:10-12	148
6:16-17	151
6:18	154

Friendly Fire

PHILIPPIANS

1:20	116
2:12-13	58
3:20-21	124

COLOSSIANS

1:25-27	63
1:27	153
2:23	228

1 TIMOTHY

2:5	62

2 TIMOTHY

2:1-2	64
3:16-17	180

TITUS

2:13	189
3:5-6	36

HEBREWS

4:15	79
4:15	152
4:15-16	137
4:15-16	180
4:16	192
7:25	94
11:1	156
11:6	65
11:6	133
12:7-11	108
13:5	92

JAMES

1:3-4	107
4:7	110
5:16	89

1 PETER

1:3-7	127
1:5	156
1:7-8	131
5:8-9	110
5:8-9	148

1 JOHN

1:9	89
3:2	124
4:4	110
5:4	110

REVELATION

12:10-12	149
22:12-13	117

Leadership Resources International

If you have been encouraged by this book, you might consider using it in a small group or class in your church. You might also consider inviting Don to teach the Bible conference "Seeing God's Sovereign Hand in Life's Journey; A Unique Look at the Life of Job," which is based on this book, in your church.

Our desire is to magnify God in the eyes of His people so that they may stand in awe, wonder and worship before Him, and be transformed in His presence. We do this as we bring the encouragement of the Scriptures to churches, pastors and missions. The largest aspect of our work is encouraging and equipping pastors in the developing world who often have little formal training for the ministry. These ministries take place throughout Latin America, China, Burma, Russia and Africa. We invite your church to partner with us in one of these training times.

For more information about our conferences or materials, contact:

Leadership Resources
12575 South Ridgeland Avenue
Palos Heights, IL 60463
(800) 980–2226
www.leadershipresources.org